"David Wood lives the lifestyle of the world traveler while contributing to thousands of people all over the world... all from his laptop. This book gives readers access to this inspired level of freedom, even those who don't think they have a business-minded bone in their body."
Michael Port, bestselling author of *Book Yourself Solid &*
Beyond Booked Solid

"Everyone is an authority in some field or another, including you. The internet has leveled the playing field so that anyone working from home (or the beach) can share their life experiences with the world and get paid for it. David makes this a no-brainer with a very clear road map that is easy and fun to follow. Enjoy the journey!"
Joel Comm, bestselling author of *The Adsense Code*

"This is not just a book but a guide for realizing your grandest dreams. With David's wisdom lighting your way, you will not only create the success you desire, you will believe in the power of the gifts you have to share with the world. The world is waiting for you; *Get Paid For Who You Are*™ will help you emerge."
Dr. Marcia Reynolds, author of *Outsmart Your Brain* and
Past President, International Coach Federation

"David Wood is a remarkable genius who knows how to have fun, make money, and make this world a better place — all at the same time. His potent and fabulous new book *Get Paid for Who You Are*™ tells the truth about what is possible when we are in tune with ourselves and the world around us. This brilliant book is a must read for anyone and everyone whose life is about making a difference. Read it, use it, share it, and thrive!"
Lynne Twist, author of *The Soul of Money*

A portion of book proceeds supports these important charities:

- Rainforest Action Network
  www.ran.org
- Byron Katie's 'The Work Foundation'
  www.theworkfoundationinc.org
- One Laptop Per Child (OLPC)
  www.laptop.org

Acknowledgment and Disclosure

Thank you to the following companies mentioned in this book for their contribution to the above charities, to me, and the idea that you can 'Get Paid For Who You Are™', through either their promotional support or affiliate commissions:

Professional Cart Solutions
Practice Pay Solutions
Weebly
Membergate
Blue Host
InfusionSoft
Ready 2 Go Articles
Instant Teleseminar
Partnership Seminar
Assessment Generator

Pages printed in the United States of America on 100% postconsumer waste recycled paper
Cover and internal design: i2i Design
First Printing: March 2010
Library of Congress Cataloging-in-Publication Data: Application in progress

ISBN: 978-1-935598-99-2
Visit the web site: www.GetPaidForWhoYouAre.com

GET PAID FOR
WHO
YOU ARE™

DAVID WOOD

PRAISE FOR *GET PAID FOR WHO YOU ARE*™

"Many people wish to help the world, but don't know the process to also *make a living from it*. David lays it out in a very simple 5 step process, making the power of the internet available even to us non-technical folks! Now you can make a contribution to your community and planet, while creating a lifestyle of freedom for yourself — it doesn't get better than that!"
John Gray, author of *Men are from Mars, Women are from Venus* - over 25 million copies sold

"The internet is still the wild, wild west for entrepreneurs. Fortunately, pioneers like David Wood arrived early and have reported back on what they've found. This book has something for absolutely anyone interested in starting a profitable online business in the shortest amount of time. David shares exactly what to do and how to do it, to catch the most exciting wave of our time."
Mike Dooley, *New York Times* Bestselling author of Infinite Possibilities, and Founder of Notes From The Universe at Tut.com

"David is a rare combination of both a brilliant internet marketer and a great visionary. His simple, proven methods will show you how to use your passion to improve lives and reach millions of people worldwide."
Marcia Wieder, Founder and CEO, *Dream University*® and *AmazingDreamers.com*

"Above the clutter of hundreds of strategies in other lifestyle books comes David Wood's elegant 5-step process - it's a simple roadmap which helps anyone quickly 'monetize' their thoughts and passions."
Alex Mandossian, CEO & Founder www.HeritageHousePublishing.com

To Michael Elam

Michael dreams of driving a bus across the US, giving free classes on Emotional Freedom Technique to communities and helping clean up their parks and rivers. He just needs to know how to fund it. This book is for Michael, and people like him, who yearn to impact the world, *and* be paid for it.

To Kathryn

Always in our hearts.

TABLE OF CONTENTS

FOREWORD

Thin and wiry, with a shock of red hair and a roguish grin, David Wood didn't look like anyone's idea of a guru. But as we sat talking together in my living room for the first time, I realized immediately he had something important to share. David has figured out how to do what most people only dream about doing their whole lives — live an abundant life while making a huge contribution, and having a blast every step of the way.

In my thirty-plus years of teaching the principles of success, I've seen that too many people are unhappy in their careers. They travel to an office every day, working 9-5 (for someone else), trading their time for money, and often at something that doesn't light them up.

Reading *Get Paid For Who You Are*™ can change all that. This book opens a door, one of realistic opportunity. If you have a passion, a hobby, a product, a service, or even your own life experience, David shows you how to reach the world with it, and to get paid for it. His system makes all of this possible — *now*! And the only person who can get in your way is also the only person who can make this happen — you!

This book is a call. A call to express. To give, influence, receive, play. To *engage*.

Will you answer the call? Is now your time? If you've been waiting to share what you truly care about with the world — and to fully receive the gifts this life has to offer — your wait is over.

Everybody's talking about the "challenging economy." And they're right, it is challenging — it's *challenging* us to play a bigger game. Are you ready? Let's begin.

JACK CANFIELD
Co-creator, *Chicken Soup for the Soul*® Series

INTRODUCTION

When a baby elephant is born in a circus, they tie its leg to a stake with a strong chain. Over time, they gradually reduce the thickness of the chain until a full-grown elephant is "held" by a flimsy piece of rope. The elephant is tied to a stake because it believes it is. What do you believe?

You could say a lifestyle of complete freedom, contribution and abundance isn't possible for you, or you can test the strength of your rope.

With your permission, I'll show you how to create a lifestyle of contribution and creativity, with financial and location freedom. Inside this book you will learn the five-step process that I used to create this lifestyle, impacting over 100,000 people and funding my travels and adventures, through an automated helping-the-world business. You'll learn the same process that is now helping thousands of people to ditch their nine to five jobs and create the lifestyle they dream of — even if they're non-technical or time-scarce.

I'll show you how to get paid for what you know and love.

I'll show you...
how to get paid...
for who you are.

You Have so Much to Share

Your passion, hobby, skill or life experience is valuable — literally. Whether it's being married, or getting divorced. Whether having a child, or losing someone dear to you — it's valuable. Whether you like stamp collecting, investing, riding horses, parenting or catering. Maybe you created a million dollar business, or failed at three start-ups. Perhaps you simply found a way to stick to your diet, or handle an angry spouse or upset child, or make pottery, or can help people find a fishing guide, or any of a myriad of skills, interests, or abilities — it's all valuable.

If you already have a business, you'll be happy to know this process is powerful for anyone with a product or service: professionals, small business owners, chiropractors, dentists, florists, potters, inventors. You can make more revenue and work less.

Now, I'm not promising you'll make internet millions. It took hard work for me to reach $40,000 a month. I also won't promise you a "4-Hour Work Week". The author of that book and I work many more hours than that, although it's entirely by choice. While it is completely possible to make a fortune and never work again by following the steps in this book, it's also normal if you have some healthy skepticism. And I know not everyone wants to aim that high.

So let's take a look at more down to earth goals that are easier to wrap the mind around.

How would your life be enhanced if you made an extra $3,000 per month while keeping your day job?

How would it feel to cut back to a job working only two or three days a week because your "how to" CD or book is starting to sell really well?

What would it be worth to you to transition to doing something you really care about and receive five testimonials a week from people you have helped?

I Was Where You Are Too

If you are working 9 to 5 for someone else at something you're not passionate about, or struggling to get more clients for your own business, then I can tell you I understand. I've been in those places not too long ago.

I was a consulting actuary for Fortune 500 companies based in New York. By all measures, I was a success. I had gone to school to learn a great profession, worked hard to get promoted, and had taken 8 years to qualify as an actuary (no small feat). I was making good money. I'd moved from Australia to my dream destination, New York City. My parents were proud and my friends thought I had it made.

But I couldn't shake the feeling that this just wasn't me!

After much soul-searching, I took six months off to pursue a life-long dream of playing guitar and singing in pubs. I dressed up in fun, silly costumes like a kilt and a long blond ABBA wig, and sang party songs like Blame It On The Boogie.

You know what? I never made it back to corporate life. I'd broken my old thought patterns and started coaching people to achieve their goals. Soon other coaches were asking me how to attract clients using the internet. I was now doing what I loved, but I was still working five days a week. So I turned my knowledge and passion into a CD product. Now I was helping people 24/7, *without* using my time!

I took many deep breaths the day I slowly wrote my resignation letter to the Institute of Actuaries of Australia. My mind was screaming, "You've invested eight years of sweat, stress and tears in qualifying — you're crazy to let that go!" But I was letting go of the old to create the new, so it felt right. I made my own choices. And that's what I want for you.

People ask me, "What is it that you do?" and the answer changes every time. For many it doesn't fit into their paradigm of what they expect to hear.

I work from my laptop wherever I am.
I create and sell information products in 49 countries using the internet.
I work from home as often as I like.
I can take three months off work when I choose.
I'm a speaker, a writer, a trainer.
I'm a traveler having fun with my friends.
I have the great satisfaction and fulfillment of helping people.

It's a life you can have. That's all I'm saying. Read on.

Chapter 1

YES, EVEN **YOU** CAN DO IT

When Jillian Wells became wheelchair bound, she felt the despair of anyone whose freedom and independence is limited. Yet she was the sort of person to do whatever she could, no matter what, and she began to devour all she could read or hear about new ventures to enrich her life.

She wanted to run online forums on self-development for women, but she had no business experience or knowledge of computers. What she did have was lots of determination and a willingness to make it happen. She began by borrowing her business partner's website, and started advertising on Facebook and e-academy. The online forums she created were deeply satisfying and transforming — for the women who attended, and for *her*.

Her other passion is running a lighthouse in Australia with guest accommodations. The lighthouse website was very old, so she contacted the web designer and reworked the entire site to make it more interactive (www.pointhicks.com.au). As a result, she is getting at least four enquiries a day, which translates into more bookings. She's the first to admit, "My lifestyle has greatly improved and I feel I'm making a difference for others and myself."

Meanwhile in Vermont, for 18 years Vicki Hoefle had taught six-week parenting classes that changed lives. As she approached retirement, it occurred to her that by filming the class, she could create a product to sell online which would fulfill two goals: create a passive income stream and enable her to travel to see her kids once they left home. She had no start-up money and no internet or marketing experience. She was also raising five teenagers at the time.

In her words, "I began by writing a basic business plan and my product began to take shape. I took every training program I could afford and I hired people to help me. Together with my partner and team, we developed a multi-media product (video, audio and workbook) with a one-year membership to an online forum. In less than a year, we increased our database from 500 to 1200 people. Our income rose from $26,000 a year to $75,000 a year in less than two years. In the last six months, we have expanded our customer base from Vermont to all of the U.S. and into Canada, and I just started my personal blog (www.parentingontrack.com). I have wonderful new relationships with people I never would have met had I not expanded my work in this direction. I love knowing that I am changing lives today, which will impact the next generation of leaders."

Vicki's advice? "Ask a million questions and then ask some more. Know that you will make countless mistakes and that's OK. And surround yourself with people who are smarter, funnier, cuter and richer than you are."

Thousands of people are every day turning what excites them into a fun and productive business which lets them either quit their day jobs or create an additional revenue stream in their lives. You could be one of them.

What might your life look like?

For a moment, imagine yourself sharing your gifts or interests or skills with the world and then...

And then...

And then...

(Are you ready?)

...imagine it happening without requiring your time or physical presence.

Imagine that while you're out on a walk, shopping, or taking a yoga class, someone is downloading your ebook in Australia. Imagine that during a month-long holiday with your family and friends in Costa Rica, people across Europe buy 2,000 copies of your new "how to" CD and publishers are reaching out to you with book deals.

What I'm talking about here is how your life could be if you take advantage of the exploding revenue possibilities by starting an internet-based business as your primary or secondary source of revenue. The lifestyle I'm describing is so new and such an unusual concept that we need a new term to describe it. What do you call people who share their gifts with thousands and then automate that sharing so they are free to work or play, travel whenever they like and live wherever they wish? Perhaps we simply call them... free.

THE FOUR FREEDOMS

You can create a lifestyle of:

Location Freedom

The ability to live or travel anywhere in the world, including the simple joy of working from home.

Time Freedom

Being able to choose to work five days a week, or one.

Financial Freedom

Not having to check the prices when you buy things that bring joy to you and those you love and not having to worry about money again.

Inner Freedom

The freedom to be yourself, and to share what you know and love with the world.

WHICH FREEDOMS WILL YOU CREATE?

You may want more time, to be closer to your family, financial abundance, creative expression, or a combination of freedoms. Which freedom is most important to you?

Jon is a good earner and saver, and he likes the large amount of vacation time his corporate accounting job offers. However, he'd love to work from a home office or while traveling, rather than being confined to a cube at work. A website presence could lead to location freedom for him.

Janet earns a good living as a landscape architect. She also feels that two weeks of travel a year is plenty. But she'd like to cut her work hours from 40 to 20 per week, to spend more time with her family. An internet business can give her time freedom.

Trent Hamm, who you're going to hear about in a little while, felt the financial wolves howling at his door, and do you know what? Today he has financial freedom, and he created it. That could be you.

Or take someone like Chris Lehner. He likes to go fishing. So he made a web page (www.walleyehunter.com) and shares fishing reports, articles, specialty coverage of topics like ice fishing, and his site gathers quite a bit of advertising. The guy's sharing something he loves with the world. How's that for inner freedom?

We all have different goals and desires. What's exciting is that you get to create the freedom that's important to you.

Freedom Ninja says: From time to time you'll see a Ninja icon like this one on the left. This one signifies an advanced tip that you can ignore if you're just starting out. The baby ninja icon is particularly for beginners. When there's a lot of information, the baby ninja will tell you where to start.

THE FREEDOM QUIZ

Let's explore how you're doing already. As you work your way through the following quiz, don't worry about your scores, since the numbers aren't important. Whether you score 10 or 70, the real question is: What can you do to add 20 points to your score over the next six months? You're also welcome to tweak the quiz to the one *you* would write.

For each statement below, give yourself a 0 if the statement is totally untrue, 5 if it's completely true and 1 through 4 for anything in between.

LOCATION FREEDOM

___ (0-5) I work in a corporate office two days a week or less.

___ (0-5) Out of the entire world, I'm living in one of my top three preferred cities.

___ (0-5) If I choose, I can easily be away from my home town for one month per year.

___ (0-5) If I choose, I can easily be away from my home town for six months per year.

___ **Total (max 20)**

TIME FREEDOM

___ (0-5) I can and do take at least four weeks a year of vacation.

___ (0-5) I can and do take at least 10 weeks a year of vacation (or I love the work that I do).

___ (0-5) I work no more than three days a week.

___ (0-5) I enjoy my spare time and have a fulfilling life outside of work.

___ **Total (max 20)**

FINANCIAL FREEDOM

___ (0–5) I have six months of living expenses in a savings account.

___ (0–5) I have no debt.

___ (0–5) I currently earn more than I spend (my savings are increasing).

___ (0–5) I have enough money to buy everything I need.

___ (0–5) I have enough money to buy at least 80 percent of the things that I want.

___ **Total (max 25)**

INNER FREEDOM

___ (0–5) I'm willing to tell the truth, even when I'll lose something.

___ (0–5) What I do helps others.

___ (0–5) I get to express myself, what I care about, or who I am, through my job.

___ (0–5) I love how my life *is*, rather than wishing it was different.

___ **Total (max 20)**

___ **Combined Total (max 85)**

In what areas are you the strongest? The weakest? In what areas would a change make the greatest difference in your life?

You may dream of traveling six months a year and working 10 hours a week — or more when a burst of creativity hits.

Or you may want to work from home one day a week, cut your work week to three days total and triple your vacation time from two weeks to six.

Or — perhaps you feel that inner freedom is the only freedom that matters and the rest will surely follow.

Circle the area(s) that *you* most want to improve.

IS IT OK TO HAVE SO MUCH FREEDOM?

If you're like most people, you grew up thinking you'd have to work 40 to 50 hours a week, 50 weeks a year, before you could take time off and play. In addition, you might have learned that work is something you must put up with to earn money and that loving what you do is nice but not a priority.

I hope you'll start to consider a new possibility — that maybe it's okay to work a lot less and have a lot more play in your life. In this day and age, you can actually get paid for doing something you really love. Perhaps you're already seeing that a lifestyle of freedom is possible for you and beginning to feel a growing desire to create it.

YES, YOU CAN DO IT!

Consider this. When Tina Maria's husband was diagnosed with a wheat allergy she spent months learning about how to cook for him. After cleaning out her pantry, pulling together a load of new recipes (including learning how to recreate some of his favorite dishes) she had developed a set of tips and insights on how to help her husband and her family adjust to the new lifestyle. She was neither a doctor nor a nutritionist, but she was on the front line fighting her husband's allergy and began to acquire quite a bit of expert advice to share with other families in a similar situation.

She was hesitant at first to start an interactive blog and to write her ebook because she didn't feel like an expert — but then she reminded herself that she knew more than most people and what she knew could save another family a lot of trial and error. She found friends to help her set up her website and to edit her book. She shied away from public speaking engagements but found she did very well running small counseling groups. Soon she was gathering enough varied input that she could start her own newsletter.

Despite her initial self-doubt, she successfully shared her insights, helped others and made money doing so.

THERE REALLY ARE THOUSANDS OF PEOPLE DOING THIS

Don't just take my word for it. There's an internet website called www.killerstart-ups.com that reviews fifteen new internet start-ups every single working day. That's about 4,000 start-ups every year — just the ones this site reviews — with subjects ranging from financial investments to resources for educators to evaluating TV shows to culinary tips.

The prospects are as limitless as the number of hobbies and interests you can think up. One website, www.itsthoughtful. com/lm.php is all about a community of people who want to get ideas for gifts that matter to those they care about. Someone had to think up the idea, start researching gifts, and start connecting others who are interested in the same thing. For that matter, someone had to think of starting a website reviewing new internet start-ups!

What's your passion, hobby, skill or experience? Can it be turned into a revenue stream for you? Yes it can, whether you like scrapbooking, deep sea diving, nifty new gadgets, lawn care, becoming a better parent, personal development, financial planning, or hiking in national parks. Whatever you like or love is something you can spend more time doing and make money while doing it!

YES! IT'S POSSIBLE FOR YOU

Are you ready to believe a lifestyle of freedom is possible for *you?*

Yes, it is possible. In fact, by applying the five steps I'll show you, and with persistent effort, it's actually quite likely.

You can also take the pressure off by realizing that you don't need to make $200,000 a year working zero days a week, in order to be very, very happy. Couldn't you use an extra $1,000 a month, and a deeper sense of reward and fulfillment? Imagine the impact on your life and on those around you, if you just took another step toward what is possible — being yourself, sharing what you know and receiving an increase in passive income. It would be a win for others and a win for you.

Perhaps the time has come for you to share yourself more generously and freely and make money while doing so.

Chapter 2

GET OUT OF YOUR **OWN** WAY

"Whether you think you can,
or think you can't — you're right."
HENRY FORD

When web designer Mike Hall pulled his SUV into the shadows of the tree-lined drive of a prospective client, he was about to find out that Joe Troyer, owner of the Cross Fire Archery shop, didn't even own a computer. In fact, Joe was Amish. But Joe knew that Amish or not, if people were to find out about his custom-made, hand-crafted bows, he needed a website.

Now the world can come to Joe to experience the passion of archery equipment made the old-fashioned way. He gets to spend his time lightly sanding a freshly bent bow while his website works away. . . because he hired someone to do it.

Hey, if Joe can manage to get a website (www.crossfire archery.com) up and running in a woodsy snow covered setting in Ohio without even owning a computer, you might have to think hard about any excuses that might be holding you back.

BUSTING THE 4 MYTHS

If you're already feeling gung-ho and raring to get going, you can jump straight to Chapter 3. But if there are any lingering doubts, then read on. Sometimes we can be our own worst enemy, with the only thing holding us back being our thoughts. Let's look at the most common limiting beliefs or myths and bust them wide open so that you're free to get a powerful start.

MYTH #1: I'M NOT AN EXPERT—WHO WILL LISTEN TO ME?

Doubting your qualifications, the value of your ideas, or the level of your expertise is common — so common that it keeps thousands of people paralyzed in dead-end jobs. If you can move past this one obstacle, you'll be far ahead of the pack in terms of what you can achieve.

What if I lack credibility?

Your life experiences — both positive and negative — are valuable, so you don't need to pretend to be more than who you are. If you're starting a new business, be honest with clients and let them know that you're not coming to them with 50 years of experience. Consider whether they really care. You can even invite one or two people to be your first clients, let them know what you have to offer and ask them to try your services for free in exchange for testimonials. Soon, you and they will experience the value of the knowledge within you.

If you're hanging on to the idea that you need to be perfect before you help others, consider that there will always be a group of people who are at least one step behind you, who will pay you for what you know. If you wait until you "have it all together" you might be dead before you've helped anybody.

Another way to get over fears about your credibility is to realize that you don't have to come up with everything yourself. Your job may be to take other people's expertise, package it and bring it to your clients. Think of Tina Maria, who started out knowing nothing about how to deal with her husband's allergy, but soon found she was gathering enough information to help others. Or Chris Lehner, who just loved fishing. You can share what you care about and the value you offer has nothing to do with how long you've been in business.

Need a confidence booster? For several ways you can build your credibility and confidence, see Section A in the bonus materials at the end of the book.

MYTH #2: I DON'T HAVE THE MONEY TO START A BUSINESS.

Twenty years ago starting a business required a physical store front that in turn required thousands of dollars for a security deposit, monthly rent and cash to invest in inventory. So, it's natural to associate starting a business with large up-front costs.

Those who didn't have the money to set up a store front might start a mail-order business advertising in magazines and shipping from home, or from a drop-shipper. However, it often took weeks or months of trial and error to find the right advertisement or magazine to reach your customers.

Now, with millions of customers surfing the internet, buying and downloading information at the click of a mouse, the landscape has changed. The internet is a viable — and cheap — store front and to get started, you need very little investment.

To get started with an internet-based company, you need:

- Internet access ($30/month)
- A computer (secondhand laptops sell for as little as $200)
- Phone (you probably have one already, or you can now make calls over the internet very cheaply)

As you can see, these costs are super low, and, if you already have a computer, phone, and internet access, your start-up costs would be *zero*. Even if you don't have these tools and you don't have the little needed to get started, you could go to your local library and use their computers for free!

Another option would be to drop other expenses. You might think, "But I need those things." Well, do you really want freedom? Then drop the car and take a bus. Carpool. Get rid of your mobile phone. Drop your gym membership and go jogging. I bet you can find at least one thing that you could drop in exchange for greater freedom.

Is it OK to make a lot of money?

Deep down you may not want to start a business for fear that people will think you're greedy or involved in a "get rich quick" scheme. If that's what you're worried about, is it really more noble for you to hide your gifts and talents than to make them available to others?

Here's an example. Let's say you're a counselor who's really good at helping women over 45 move through the process of divorce. A woman comes to your website lost, anxious, depressed and panicked about what life might be like after divorce. Even though she knows it's the right decision, she doesn't have the courage to divorce because it's too scary and she can't see the way forward. As she gets information from your website she begins to feel some comfort, peace and optimism; she begins to create some goals for herself.

Then, she subscribes to your newsletter and after two to three months she has received so much from your free tips that she's ready to proceed with her divorce. So, she spends $47 on your ebook, downloads it and devours it in about five hours. She's so excited and happy, she follows your action steps and she starts putting them into place. She's empowered. A month later, she calls you up and says, "I'd like to hire you. I've saved up the money and I'd like to work with you." So you work with her over the phone and support her through the process of achieving her goal.

Perhaps making money is a normal, healthy byproduct of helping others.

MYTH #3: I DON'T HAVE TIME TO START A BUSINESS.

If you want to start a new business, you'll need to invest time. At a minimum I suggest seven hours a week, or one hour a night. That won't threaten your day job or require you to quit.

If seven hours feels like too much for you, given your current schedule, scale back other activities. What are you willing to drop? If you say, "Nothing" ask yourself: Is a lifestyle of freedom important to me? If it is, get up early, stay up late, or say "No" to some activities that don't fulfill you anyway. You can also consider:

- Take time off work, either paid or unpaid, to get your business rolling
- Negotiate with your boss to work four days a week, perhaps doing a trial period first and being open to taking a 20 percent cut in pay
- If your boss won't entertain a reduction in your hours, find an employer who will
- Work weekends
- Partner with someone who has more time to devote to the business
- Give up TV

In other words, there are *many* solutions, if your desire for a lifestyle of freedom is strong enough.

If I was starting again, I would work each night of the week *and* take a day a week — Saturday or Sunday — called "Internet Day," on which I turned off my phones, asked friends and family to respect the time I'm investing in the business, and then, when the day is up, showed my appreciation by taking them to dinner and celebrating the fact that I'm one step closer to achieving my dream.

MYTH #4: I NEED BUSINESS OR TECHNICAL SKILLS

Let's tackle business skills first.

You may be asking yourself, "If I start a business, don't I *need* to be naturally good at business?"

The answer is No. But it's a really good question, and here's why.

There are many people who go into business for themselves without help. They think they can do everything — including balancing the books, making sales calls and hiring employees — even if these were previously their weak spots. They may reach out for help by hiring cheap, inexperienced staff, but if the business owner doesn't know what he or she is doing, training the staff creates whole new problems.

There are two ways to get around this. The first is to train yourself in business. One quick way to do that is to read *The E-Myth* by Michael Gerber. It's simply the bible of internet business, hands down, and it showed me what a business really is, in language that anyone can understand.

The second is to partner with someone who *does* know business. This tip is worth thousands of dollars and may save you years of pain, but it's not really rocket science is it? If you're short on business experience, get someone long on business experience to balance you out. We'll explore that strategy more later.

"But if they run the business, what am I doing?" you may ask.

Perhaps you're the talent. You're the person creating the solutions for people facing divorce, or bankruptcy, or having a child, or a thousand other possible life challenges. You're the inspiration, the driving force, the person who remembers the vision when things get tough. Maybe you're the people person who can get that new employee to stay, or the one who can land the alliance with a big mailing list because you just plain enjoy developing partnerships with people. Or maybe you're the one who's good at massage, hairdressing, tennis, or raising children.

Now that I've laid all of that out on the table, let me take the pressure off a bit. You'll be relieved to know that an information/internet driven business requires far less time, energy and knowledge to succeed than a traditional brick-and-mortar business.

Now let's talk about technical skills.

Just as with business skills and practices, many of us do not naturally gel with computers and other electronic tools. While some people find e-mail, Facebook and blogging easy to learn, others are more comfortable away from the computer.

Fortunately, as odd as it might seem, you don't need to be web-savvy to run a successful internet-based business. You have two options:

- Partner with someone who is technical-minded, or
- Invest the time to learn the important computer skills.

I'll bet that you already have at least 50 percent of the computer skills you'll need to run a successful internet business — including the ability to start-up and shut down a computer, send and receive email and attachments and conduct searches using Google. There are many free and public resources that will help you beef up your computer expertise.

And remember Amish Joe, who didn't know a thing about building a website?

But aren't there other skills I'll need?

Sure. Again, you'll learn them or outsource them. For example, one important skill is writing. If that doesn't come naturally to you, draft a list of questions people often ask you and write down your answers. You'll find that within a very short time, you'll naturally come up with enough content to populate your website and newsletters. You will be amazed at what flows out of you and how good it feels to share it.

If you're still skeptical or hesitant to write, you can hire someone to write for you, ask a friend to interview you and transcribe the interview, or borrow content from someone else's website with a promise to provide credit. Remember: "perfect" writing and speaking skills are not a prerequisite for sharing your gifts with the world.

MOVING RIGHT ALONG

In the next chapter you'll begin the "how-to" portion of the process with your first big step as you identify your niche or interest area and consider WHO you will help.

RESOURCES

- See "Your Confidence Booster" in Section A in the back of the book for tips on how to build your credibility and confidence.

Chapter 3

STEP 1: DECIDE **WHO** YOU HELP

As Trent Hamm tells it, "I sat at the kitchen table flipping through the mail, seeing bill after bill after bill. I tore open a couple of them immediately, wanting to see the terrible news in its full glory. I began to calculate what I could afford to pay and what I could not. I began to quickly realize that the pile of bills I just received not only wouldn't be covered by the current balance of my checking account, but that my next paycheck would not cover them either — and that was if I spent absolutely nothing on food, gasoline, or anything else."

"I sat there completely stunned for a moment. Then I got up and went into my son's room, closed the door behind me and sat down in the rocking chair across from his crib. He was so tiny laying there, less than six months old, and sleeping so peacefully there without a worry in the world. As I watched him lay there, gently breathing, emotions poured through me. Guilt. Shame. Embarrassment. Pain."

"I was failing this wonderful little boy, this child who had already brought incalculable joy into my life. He relied on me for everything and because of my poor decision-making and my selfishness, I was letting him down. I closed my eyes and didn't realize at first I was crying, almost uncontrollably. My wife came in and put her arm around me. Eventually my sobbing woke up my son, who also began to cry. Sarah held us both."

Trent was, as you may also be, at a crossroads, but he then decided on the path toward action. Hear him out: "I buried myself in personal finance books, coupling them with the philosophy and economics books I had already been reading. Over the next few months, I started to take some radical steps to fix our financial state."

"More importantly, I began to realize that this entire experience was one that other people were struggling with. How can a person balance all of the aspects of modern life on a limited income? How can we find personal and professional happiness in an increasingly complex world where real wages for most of us haven't changed in decades?"

"So, in October 2006, I started (www.thesimpledollar.com) on my own with no fanfare in order to share these experiences. Within two months, I had 100,000 visitors. Today, The Simple Dollar has nearly a million visitors a month and tens of thousands more who receive articles by email."

"Along the way, I've had conversations with thousands of people who were struggling with questions like these in their own lives. I've heard countless stories of people digging through the challenging connections between their money, their happiness, their daily choices and their mission in life."

WHY TARGETING IS CRITICAL

Until you're clear on your target market, it's too easy to wander aimlessly, _wanting_ to help, but unable to. It's like trying to run with your shoelaces tied together. When you are clear on who you want to help — your "target market" — you'll want to tell everyone who'll listen and forge ahead with energy.

A target market or niche is the group of people you've decided to help. You can narrow it down in lots of cool ways, including age, income, where they live, occupation, or what they need. A target market is very specific and helps you to focus your marketing efforts. Without it you can get too scattered to succeed.

Many people ask, "Why do I need a target market? Why can't I offer my services to everyone?" After all, why would anyone want to turn away customers? It can feel limiting.

However, choosing a niche or group of people to focus on doesn't keep you from working with other people outside of your niche. You're still allowed to work with others when they come to you. Surprisingly, it increases the number of people who come to you because you're more attractive; you're clear, focused, working with the right clients and happy. More importantly, it makes it so much easier for the right clients to find you!

For example — you can happily serve everyone who drives into your gas station. But you need something clear and specific like "Serving veterans since 1985" on the billboard out the front.

To take another example, say you're an accountant who owns your own business, and you're looking for a coach to help take your business to the next level. Who would you most likely sign up with: a general business coach, or one who specializes in helping accountants build profitable businesses? Intuitively you can see that someone who specializes is more attractive!

Your own experience probably shows you that you are not attracted to products or services designed to help "everyone". If you're a woman, don't you prefer bath products that are designed for women? It's the same for your customers: people like to purchase solutions that are specific to their problem.

In addition, if your target market is "everyone", how do you reach *everyone*? Do you have the money to advertise on network television? Do you have hundreds of thousands of dollars to place advertisements in *USA Today?*

On the other hand, what if you are a business coach who helps accountants grow profitable businesses? Knowing your target market, you home in on them through accounting magazines, at CPA conferences, or even through local stores that stock accounting office supplies.

Another problem with not having a clear target market is that you can't be remembered and referred. People can't pass the word about what you do if even you can't tell them. Have a sexy statement that sizzles and they'll be able to tell the world.

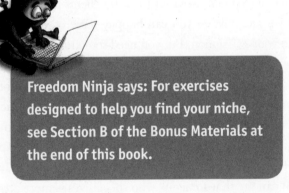

Freedom Ninja says: For exercises designed to help you find your niche, see Section B of the Bonus Materials at the end of this book.

ACTION TIME: YOUR FREEDOM BUDDY

Reading this book won't change your life. Applying it will.

Chapters 1 and 2 involved reading only, but moving forward you will be both reading and working. You'll want support in your new venture, so it's time to line up a FREEDOM BUDDY — a friend, spouse or colleague who is also reading and working through this book. This can make the difference between you using the book to create a life of freedom, versus using it for entertainment. Set up a weekly time to talk as you each work through your own copy of the book. For tips on setting up this relationship powerfully, go to www.GetPaidForWhoYouAre.com/buddy. You'll be glad you have someone in your corner. I urge you to lean on each other often as you forge ahead.

Freedom Ninja says: Lining up your Freedom Buddy to support you along the way is the single most important action you can take in this book, so go and make some phone calls and emails right now and line up someone to share this journey with you. Who would you love an excuse to spend more time with, who also wants to reach the world with something they have to share? They could be a partner in your business, or be creating their own.

Also, as you go through each chapter, schedule time in your diary to complete the action steps — starting with scheduling the 2-3 hours you'll need to complete the actions of this chapter. Make a promise to yourself to do them. And congratulate yourself for making freedom a priority in your life!

HOW TO CRAFT A SIZZLING ELEVATOR PITCH

Now it's time to refine your offer and target market into an "elevator pitch". An elevator pitch is you telling someone what you do in the time it takes to ride an elevator. Sometimes 10-30 seconds is all you'll have to state who you are and what you can do.

The beauty of an elevator pitch is that, in addition to helping you say with ease and confidence what you do and for whom, it also allows others to spread the word about you. So, the next time someone asks your friend, "What does Mollie do?" Your friend replies, "She helps small business owners get free publicity". Or, "She teaches families of cancer patients how to support their loved one and cope".

Now it's your turn. What do (or will) you do and for whom? Write down your elevator pitch using the following formula: *I help Y with X.*

If it's not sizzling, you could ask yourself, "Is my target market too broad?" For example, you might say, "I help businesses with team communication." That's true, but what type of businesses? Established ones? Start-ups? In what industry?

"Oh," you say. "I get it. I help start-up biotech companies with team communication." That is better and I know you help the team communicate, but what problem does this solve? What is the result you are helping these companies to achieve?

"They are able to get past their personal conflicts and work together to bring products to market faster, and those products save lives."

Great! Then say that.

"Okay. How about: I help start-up biotech companies bring life-saving drugs to market faster."

Wonderful. That would leave me asking you how you do that, which would be your entrée to talking about improving team communication and how it can improve results.

Do you see how it works? This is a perfect exercise to engage in with a Freedom Buddy. Test your elevator pitches on each other as well as with your family and friends and embrace their feedback. Each piece of feedback can help you to hone your elevator pitch and really make it sing.

Elevator pitches

Here are more samples of "sizzling" elevator pitches:

> I help start-up biotech companies bring life-saving drugs to market faster.
> I show you how to make pottery at home in 5 easy steps.
> I help women 45 and older recover from divorce.
> I help people who need to buy or sell used heavy machinery.
> I show people how to save thousands of dollars on their plumbing expenses, by doing it themselves.
> I connect hikers with the trails just made for them.
> I teach how to make jewelry you love.

A Freedom Ninja reminder: Don't spend too much energy trying to get the "right" niche. It's more important to bite the bullet and move forward with a niche that *could* feel good. You'll learn much more if you proceed with what you have than if you wait for Moses to come down from the mountain with your niche written on a tablet of stone.

CREATING A TAGLINE AND BUSINESS NAME

Now that you have your elevator pitch and can communicate what you do, read through it again to pinpoint the one or two words that sum up the essence of your business and the value that you bring.

For example, the elevator pitch "I help start-up biotech companies bring life-saving drugs to market faster" might use the tagline of "Communication that saves lives". The elevator pitch "I help empty-nester women rediscover their purpose" might choose the business name "My Second Life".

Just as you did with your elevator pitch, play with words and phrases. For more ideas, use a thesaurus and also review your Take Inventory worksheet if you used one in the Bonus Materials in Section B at the back of the book, and any other notes you made. It's also fun to search online for your potential business names, tag lines, or elevator pitches and see what other sites pop up. Review other websites, logos, banners, taglines and newsletter titles until you find some sizzle of your own. Keep massaging

Freedom Ninja says: It's easy to expect blinding clarity in the first couple of days and then feel disappointed if it doesn't come. Sometimes it's as simple as a feeling that one group might be fun to work with. Be willing to try out this group or target market, knowing that you'll find out soon enough if it's the right one for you. If not, you might learn enough to know what group to try next.

the business name and tagline until you come up with one that resonates with you and connects to your passion!

Your business name should meet as many of the following criteria as possible, bearing in mind that it's rarely possible to satisfy all of them:

- You are excited to tell people about it
- It gives a sense of who you help and/or what problem you help them with
- It's simple, short and memorable
- It contains at least one word that your potential customers would be searching for on the internet (known as keywords). For example, if you sell baskets, then having baskets in the name is important.
- The domain name is available. This means no-one has already taken this name for their website. You can check this at www.GoDaddy.com. We'll discuss this in more detail in Chapter 4.

For example, let's say Paul chooses the name "My Second Life" for his divorce-consulting business. This name meets the first few criteria: he loves it, it's easy to remember, it describes his service of offering a new life to women going through divorce, and it's simple, short and easy to remember. It misses out on one criteria as it doesn't include words people are likely to be searching for such as "survive divorce". But that's fine — it's hard to satisfy all the criteria.

DO I HAVE TO SAY "NO" TO CLIENTS OUTSIDE OF MY NICHE?

If someone approaches you from outside of your niche and wants to work with you, by all means consider it! Just because you focus on helping women 45 and older recover from divorce doesn't mean that someone who is 37 won't benefit from working with you. These are the sorts of things you discuss with your Freedom Buddy. You'll find the world overlaps far more than you think and chances to help and create freedom at the same time are everywhere!

GETTING FURTHER HELP

Hey, don't look now, but there are several bonus chapters, a dozen worksheets, a few videos, the occasional interview and a bunch of Expansion Modules that couldn't possibly fit here in the book. So I put what I could in the bonus section in the back of the book and have made the rest — called "Get Paid University" — available online for a low monthly access fee. As an owner of this book, you can enter the coupon code "freedom" to get the first month for free, giving you access to many of the resources listed in this book. I suggest you do so. At the end of each chapter I'll point to further tools and resources within Get Paid University, as well as other useful resources available elsewhere on the net.

RESOURCES

See More on "Decide WHO You Help" in Section B in the back of the book for exercises to help you determine your target market

- For tips on setting up your Freedom Buddy relationship, go to www.GetPaidForWhoYouAre.com/buddy
- **Get Paid University**
  (www.GetPaidForWhoYouAre.com/access)
  - "Take Inventory" Worksheet
  - "Decide WHO You Help" Expansion Module
  - "Define Your Market" worksheet

Chapter 4

STEP 2: SET UP YOUR WEBSITE IN **SEVEN DAYS**

After working thirty-seven years for Pacific Bell, Robert Medak, of Osborne, Kansas, was ready to work for himself. He craved doing something with meaning that used his creativity and earned him some extra money. So he decided to start an online business writing articles and book reviews, as well as editing and proofreading. To do that, he would need an internet website. Though he had some computer knowledge, he's the first to admit he's not "a computer geek". He says, "I would rate my skills between novice and intermediate. There is still a good deal for me to learn about computers."

Once he had committed to getting a website going, he realized there are three basic choices to start a website:

- Do it all yourself from scratch
- Get a host that makes the more difficult steps easier during creation and maintenance

- Hire someone to set up your site for you, and even adjust the content as needed

He chose the middle ground, which allows him hands-on access, and says, "I maintain my site, add things to it and try to update the content or rearrange it as I learn more or add content, like other sites I wish to link to from my website."

He understands why most people feel overwhelmed at the thought of initiating their first web page. He says, "Many people get flustered because there is so much information and so many people saying your website needs this or that. It's your site; make it the way you want it, not what people say it should be."

"Do I need a blog or a normal website?" Freedom Ninja says: Ultimately you'll probably want both. A nice professional website is a place to put the key information you want potential customers to read, and to guide them through it in a particular order. A blog is a place to put random spontaneous thoughts, in a format that shows recent material first. Blogs are very popular with search engines. But don't sweat the decision — it's easy to have both. Your web designer can easily add a blog to your website, or a few standard web pages to your blog.

It is easier than most people think. Don't get fooled into thinking you need to be a web designer to create a website. It just isn't true."

When he first saw his website (www.stormywriter.com) up and running on the internet and started to get results from it he felt a surge of warmth that rippled all the way down to the toes in his lounging moccasins, a warmth that said to him, "I am a professional."

GETTING YOUR OWN WEBSITE UP AND RUNNING

You *don't* have to spend a year building a fancy site when three pages will do just fine for now, and you can do that in a week. Your goal in Step 2 is to get your website up and running *fast*, because the faster people can find you, the faster you can help them *and* get paid for it. And you'll keep your momentum up as you build your machine to serve the world.

Now let's get into the really fun stuff!

1) Choose a Design That's Right for You

Before we start on building your site, think about the "look and feel" of your website. Do you want your website to be packed with information or spacious and elegant? What is the mood that you want people to feel: hopeful and motivated to take action, or peaceful — knowing everything will be okay?

For instance, Leanne Ely's menu planning solution site (www.savingdinner.com) has a breezy cheerful style with a superhero-dressed shopper flying along behind a loaded grocery cart.

That wouldn't work as well for Anette Meier, who makes baskets by hand and markets them on her site (www.ahmbaskets.com). For her, an artsy look and font function better.

For Mort Fertel, who has a marriage fitness site (www.marriagemax.com), a business-like font accompanies an understanding looking face and a hand clearly wearing a wedding ring.

Take a moment right now to write down what you'd like your customer to feel when he or she comes to your site.

Now it's time to surf the web to find other sites that mesh with what you're looking for. Which sites appeal to you? Or do any of their *elements* appeal to you? You might find one website that makes you say, "I want those colors!" and another that makes you feel, "I like the simplicity — it's very elegant." You might find yet another and think to yourself, "I like how there's a border around the whole site." Make notes that you'll be able to give to the designer who will design your site if you don't intend to do the mechanics of design yourself.

Also, take a look at the images on the sites and if you like any of them, right-click the image, select "Save Target As," and save the image to your hard drive. This doesn't mean you'll use that exact image — especially if it's copyrighted — but you can show it to your designer so they know what you're looking for. For example, you might realize that you want to use a silhouette of a woman leaping for joy on the beach to give customers a sense of what it feels like to work with you. When you're ready to buy an image, go to www.istockphoto.com, where you can buy the rights to use an image for as little as one dollar.

During your browsing, you'll also want to save logos you like. Obviously you won't use other businesses' logos, but you may find a logo that you could use as a template for your own — one that has a typeface you like or a symbol you'd like to incorporate. Keep it in your file and when the time is right, share it with your designer to give them an idea of what you want your own logo to look and feel like.

Once you have all this information, a fun, cool way to develop your site is to create a design competition using www.99designs.com or www.crowdspring.com. This involves getting say 15 people to create a competing design for your site, with your prize (e.g., $300) being awarded to the best one. Here's what my friend Josh Hood got when he was willing to put up $750:

Take a moment to check in with yourself or your Freedom Buddy. Have you locked in a date for when you'll finish Step 2? Have you set aside "freedom-building" time? Go and schedule at least 3-4 hours right now to start applying these great actions.

Freedom Ninja asks: "Does your website feel like *you?*" Coach Joelle Prochera says, "Listen to your gut, and be honest about what you do and don't like. You'll know if something has too much energy or is too blah, if the color makes you uneasy or if the picture speaks to your soul. Be willing to trust yourself." See how she did it at www.CoachJoelle.com.

You could do a really rough version in as little as 3-4 hours. But 14 hours is probably more realistic to arrive at something you're really happy with. You can always come back later and make improvements.

Do you realize you're taking another step toward greater location, time, financial and inner freedom? Perhaps it's time for a quiet pat on the back.

2) The Three Pages You Need

I want you to get your website up and running quickly, so we're going to start with the three essential pages your website needs now (the rest can come weeks or even months down the track):

The Welcome Page

About Me / Contact Page

Products and Services Page

The Welcome Page. The purpose of the welcome page, also called your home page, is to let your customers know that they've come to the right place because you can help them.

On this page you'll want to include:

- Who you help
- The problem(s) you solve
- The benefits you provide
- Why they should choose you!

About Me / Contact Page. In the About Me page of your website you can go into more detail about your background by providing a rough bio. Some key points to mention are:

- Your relevant experience
- Your passion for your subject
- Any cool results you've achieved for your own life or business, or for your clients
- Anything else that adds to your credibility
- A testimonial or two

Services and Products Page. This page should display the goods or services you offer. If you provide a service it helps customers feel more comfortable about working with you because they'll have an idea of what the process will be like. If you're a consultant for biotech companies, you may want to outline your process so companies know what to expect. They'll see that you understand their business and have put a lot of thought into how to solve their problems. If you make a product, list the benefits and features. Write one or two paragraphs about your offer, with the aim of having visitors to your site contact you.

Freedom Ninja has more support for building your three basic pages in Section C of the Bonus materials at the back of this book.

3) Register your website name

Your next step is to register the name of your website on the internet, also known as your *domain name.* By registering the name of your site, you are "leasing" a piece of real estate for your internet store front, so no-one else can use it.

The beauty of the internet is that this piece of real estate will cost you a *lot* less than a "physical" store front, at about $10 a year versus thousands of dollars a month. In addition, customers can reach your internet store front in seconds no matter where they are, so you can sell to people whether they're in your home-town or half-way around the world!

What should the name of your website be? It will ideally be your business name to keep it simple for you and everyone else. So, for example, if your business is called My Second Life, you would now want to register www.MySecondLife.com as your domain name.

If your business name is not available on the web (i.e., someone already has it) then it's time to get a little creative. You might try and register www.MySecondLife.net or www.MySecondLife.org (not as good because people always assume they'll find you at the .com, but you get to use a business name you love). Failing that, you might try and register www.My-Second-Life.com or www.MySecondLifeNow.com. If your company is based outside of the United States, make sure to register your domain name under your country's suffix as well as the .com. For example, if you were based in the UK you would register www.MySecondLife.co.uk and www.MySecondLife.com if you can get them both.

If all versions of your chosen name are taken, maybe you can still buy it from the owner — especially if they aren't doing much with it. For example, I paid $1,500 for the www.solutionbox.com domain name, because I had my heart set on it. Go to www.whois.com to find out who has the domain and see if you can make an offer.

Finally, if all versions of your chosen name are taken *and* the current owner doesn't want to give it up, then it might be time to brainstorm a new business name. I don't recommend having a different domain name to the name of your business because you will confuse your customers and dilute your brand.

Use www.nameboy.com or www.domainexposer.com to come up with alternate naming ideas. You might like one of the names proposed, or it may spark you to go in a new direction. Whatever you do, don't worry if "your" name is taken. Reach out to your Freedom Buddy or a friend and see how you can use this challenge to come up with something even better!

Once you have a domain name or names to register, go to www.GoDaddy.com and register it for one year (should be under $13). When you're done, we'll start building your site!

5) Build your website!
Option 1: Weebly

If you can easily afford at least $500 and you know you'll want lots of customization, then you can skip ahead to Option 2 and hire a Web Wizard to build your website for you.

Chances are you are not a web designer yourself and don't have a big budget. If so, then set up a website yourself at a site like www.GoWeeblyNow.com. It's very easy to use, has powerful features, and most of it is free. You might even get away without hiring a Web Wizard to help you, but if you get stuck you can always move to Option 2.

1. Sign up for a free account at www.GoWeeblyNow.com.
2. Enter the domain you chose above as the title for your site.
3. Click on "Designs" up the top, and choose from 77 templates (You can always change it later).

4. Click on "Pages" up the top. You already have a Home page. Click on "New Page" and add an "About Us" page. Now repeat to add a "Products and Services" page. If you want to get all fancy, click on "New Blog" and add a blog so that your screen looks like this:
5. Then click "Save".

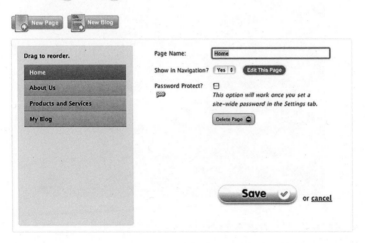

6. Click on "Home" in the menu of your site, and then drag "Paragraph with title" from the top menu onto the page, and start writing. Hint: Let yourself be guided by "The three pages you need" section earlier in this chapter, and in Section C in the back of the book. Repeat for the other two pages on your site.

7. When you're done, click "Publish" in the top right, and your first draft site will be available on the web!

As you play around you'll discover you can easily add pictures, a photo gallery, and other cool stuff. If you want to upgrade to a Pro account for under $5 per month, you can add audio and video, have multiple sites and remove the small ad at the bottom of your pages. And you'll be happy to know that whether you have a free or paid account, Weebly throws in web hosting at no charge.

> **Freedom Ninja Tip:** If you get stuck and Weebly's online support isn't doing it for you, see if you can trade some of your product or service with a friend who has some technical skills. If that doesn't cut it, or you just want more flexibility with your site, then move to Option 2.

Option 2: Hiring a Web Wizard

If you're happy with Weebly or a similar site, you might get away with waiting on hiring help for a couple of months. But even so I encourage you to get help as soon as you possibly can. If you can afford $500 for a website, tried Weebly and want more, or just need help with things like images and audio, then it's definitely time to get help. It's time to hire a Web Wizard.

A Web Wizard can:
- help you with your Weebly site
- recommend another platform (e.g., www.Wordpress.com is a great alternative to Weebly; you'll just need a bit of help setting it up)
- use a program to create your site from scratch, which has the ultimate flexibility
- edit images and audio for you

I strongly recommend you hire someone to handle all the technical details. If you love fiddling with learning new things like web design, then by all means feel free to play with making the first draft of what you need. But have a Web Wizard ready to polish the final product and bail you out when you get stuck.

Imagine how it would feel to constantly delegate all of your technical problems to someone who enjoys handling them, instead of tearing your hair out for days or weeks trying to make the tiniest steps. The fastest and easiest way to create a website is to hire someone else to do it, so you can focus on your gifts. Finding a Web Wizard is the difference between flying and crawling!

I know it can seem like a big expense to hire someone when you're just starting out. But to be successful in business, you need to know when to invest. In the case of your Web Wizard, you're probably looking at a $250 investment for a website (unless you use Weebly) as well as three to ten hours of finding, interviewing, testing and hiring the person.

Up front, that may seem like a lot to you. However, if you look at the big picture, the time you invest now could connect you to someone who will help you throughout the life of your business and can be there when you need them in a pinch. Having a good Web Wizard on call means that a problem can be fixed in a day, instead of you stewing over it for a week. Do not skimp on this process!

Your best bet for finding a Web Wizard is to ask every single person you know if they can refer someone inexpensive (say $20 per hour if you're lucky, but $30 per hour is reasonable too) and good. Failing that, you can post an ad on www.rentacoder.com, www.craigslist.com (paid ad) or www.elance.com. For a more detailed support guide on how to hire your Web Wizard, see the resources at the end of this chapter.

WEB HOSTING

If you use Weebly for your website as described above, or the basic hosted version of Wordpress, then you don't have to worry about finding a company to host your site, as they include it in their service.

However, if you don't use Weebly, or you want advanced features with Wordpress, or your Web Wizard is going to create your site from scratch using an html editor, then you or your Web Wizard will need to choose a host.

A web host is a company that houses your website for you. It gives it a place to live on the internet, and serves up the required pages when someone comes to visit.

I recommend www.BlueHostDirect.com. They are inexpensive, high quality, and I've spoken with their CEO Matt Heaton and he's passionate about providing quality and affordable hosting. It's $6.95/month for unlimited space and bandwidth with good uptime and fast phone tech support.

KEEP BACKUPS

Even if you have the world's best web host, it is important to have your Web Wizard keep a copy of your entire site, preferably in a couple of places. Then, in the event that your web host crashes or loses your data, you'll be covered.

For an inexpensive online backup service, visit www.mozy.com

GET TO IT!

Now you have everything you need to get your website up and running in seven days. Next, I'll show you how a newsletter is actually the key to this entire strategy, and how you can set yours up in seven days.

RESOURCES

- See "What to Put On Your Website" in Section C in the back of this book
- www.99designs.com or www.crowdspring.com to create a competition to see who can create the best design for you
- www.istockphoto.com — Collection of images that cost as little as $1 per image to use on your website
- www.BlueHostDirect.com — Site where you can find out whether your domain name has already been taken
- www.whois.com — Lists the current "owner" of a domain name and contact information, in case you want to buy the name
- www.nameboy.com — Offers alternate site names if yours is taken
- www.rentacoder.com — Good resource for helping you find your Web Wizard
- www.elance.com — Another good resource for finding a Web Wizard or virtual assistant
- www.craigslist.org — Community bulletin board, where you can place free ads for a Web Wizard
- www.w3schools.com/html/DEFAULT.asp — learn HTML for free
- www.mozy.com for an inexpensive online backup service

- **Get Paid University**
  (www.GetPaidForWhoYouAre.com/access)
  - Sample Bios
  - "Create My Bio" Worksheet
  - Bonus Online Chapter: Creating Coaching or Consulting Revenue — for strategies on how to sell coaching or consulting from your site
  - Web Wizard Hiring Guide (including a sample ad you can post)
  - Web Host Support Guide — for a review of the major hosting services
  - "How to Create a Website in 7 Days" Expansion Module

Chapter 5

STEP 3: SET UP YOUR NEWSLETTER IN **SEVEN DAYS**

Marissa was earning a little extra money on the side doing bookkeeping for a couple of friends. When she got laid off from her 9-5 job, she decided to use her skills to launch a proper business. She did a training course on bookkeeping, read two good business books and let her friends know she was open for business. She was pretty good at getting people's books in order — all she needed was more clients. So she started a website. Good so far.

Next she announced her bookkeeping service and fees on her site and watched two months go by without a single phone call. That's where she went wrong, horribly wrong.

GETTING IT RIGHT

Go to any website and you'll see how insane 99 percent of website owners are.

These crazy people think that in the first 30 seconds of someone browsing their site, they'll build a relationship with customers and earn enough trust to get a credit card number. It's absolutely insane and I used to do it.

I used to think, "Come to my site and pay $300 a month for my coaching." Almost everyone would visit for 30 seconds and then move on to another site, possibly never to visit my site again.

When I see my clients and students making this same mistake, I give them a new mantra: *Flowers before sex in the Bahamas.*

If you just met someone in a coffee shop, you wouldn't ask them straight away to have sex in the Bahamas would you? (Well… assuming you don't live in California). You'd start by getting to know the person, perhaps a drink, followed by dinner, some flowers and chocolates. You work up to a deeper connection. Your website should work the same way.

Freedom Ninja Tip: Your #1 website goal is to get their email address, and build a relationship by sending regular, valuable content. That's why a newsletter is so critical.

If your site says, "Hello, it's nice to meet you and now please buy my product or service," you're rushing them, and you'll lose them — perhaps forever. Given you may only have 30 seconds with this visitor, instead of asking for the purchase straight away, offer them something valuable in exchange for their email address.

This exchange often gives you permission to send them valuable content. In this way you can develop a relationship and market to your customer not just for 30 seconds but possibly for life. And not just for one product or service, but maybe dozens.

In this chapter, I'll show you how to collect visitors' email addresses and create a successful newsletter system — based on my experience of growing an email list from 25 friends to the largest coaching newsletter in the world, with 70,000 subscribers.

Freedom Ninja Tip: If you're just getting your feet wet and want to take smaller steps, here's what to focus on: just understand how critical a newsletter is and draft your very first issue.

MORE ON WHY YOU MUST HAVE A NEWSLETTER...

The number one goal of your website, if you want your list of contacts to grow quickly, is to capture your visitor's email address — like getting the phone number of a girl or guy you like, or the card of someone you meet at a conference. Then, through your newsletter, they can get to know you. You might even include personal snippets in addition to the value and advice you offer. Over time, every two weeks, 26 times a year, you can visit their inbox and earn their trust — a much stronger connection than can be achieved in one website visit. This way, you can use your newsletter to turn a 30 second website visit into a life-time relationship.

Your newsletter will help you to:

Be there when people need you. When some people visit your website, they'll be curious but not ready to buy. If all you have is a website, they'll satisfy their curiosity and move on. But if they subscribe to your newsletter, chances are your name will be top of mind, or your newsletter will hit their Inbox, just when they need you and are ready to take the next step.

Increase referrals. When you send out newsletters, your customers do some of your marketing for you by forwarding your newsletters to friends. It's a referral system that requires no extra effort from you.

Free up your time. One of the big benefits of having a newsletter is that *it* works while *you* sleep. When a customer comes to your website and subscribes to your newsletter you won't even know about it. The same goes for payment. If you charge for your newsletter, payment happens automatically. You won't know about it until you see the deposit to your bank account. You can also automate the delivery of your newsletter. If you're using an "auto responder" (which I'll talk about later) you won't even know your newsletter has gone out except for the influx of sales and money rolling into your bank account.

Cut your costs. Imagine how much it would cost me to mail postcards to 70,000 people in 90 countries or — even crazier — call all of them. I'd have to pay thousands of dollars in printing and shipping, not to mention the "cost" to the trees. But how much does it cost me to send an ezine (internet magazine) to 70,000 people this afternoon? Zero (given I pay a fixed annual cost for my newsletter service).

Create an instant market for new products or services. A newsletter database gives you a built-in market for any new product or service you develop. I built my newsletter for three years without having a product to sell. When I developed my first MP3 (a format for compressing audio) product, I told my newsletter subscribers and received $5,000 in sales in 48 hours. It was very exciting!

Research and Develop. You can invite newsletter subscribers to be part of your core feedback loop. Typically at least a few people will volunteer, giving you a group of researchers who offer a deeper level of feedback on whether your newsletter content is valuable, as well as what features that they would like to see in new products.

Build an asset for your business. Here's the wildest thing about your newsletter database: it becomes an asset for your business that you can trade. As your database grows, people who are big in your industry will seek you out. They'll want you to promote their stuff and they'll promote yours in return. It's the biggest secret about having a newsletter.

Freedom Ninja says: Whoa, there! Pause and read that last reason for having a newsletter again. It's the single most important item on the list. You are creating something of immense value!

Are you ready to get your newsletter rolling? Great!

YOUR NEXT SEVEN DAYS

You can get your newsletter system set up in the next seven days if you stay focused. You just need to read this chapter, follow the steps and work with your Freedom Buddy for extra support.

In your plan, you could break up your work like this:

    Day 1 – Create a "free download" (the ethical bait)

    Day 2 – Set up your newsletter system

    Day 3 – Put a signup form on your website

    Day 4 – Convert your current contacts to subscribers

    Day 5 – Choose your newsletter design (template)

Day 6 – Draft your first issue

Day 7 – Send it out!

If you're working with a Web Wizard it's even easier.

DAY 1 - CREATE A "FREE DOWNLOAD"

To get a website visitor to give you his email address, you've got to offer something in return. This could easily increase your subscription rate by 50%! Remember, flowers before sex in the Bahamas! Your "flower" is a freebie download. Once upon a time you could simply offer a free subscription to your newsletter, but free newsletters are everywhere and too many of us have been burned by spammers to hand over our email addresses without receiving something of greater value in return.

How to Create Your Freebie:

With your target market in mind, write the "Top Ten Tips on How to [Insert Your Topic]," for example, "The Top Ten Ways to Double Your Energy." What questions does your target market ask you over and over? What mistakes do they often make? This Top Ten tips document will be your free download that *comes with* a free subscription to your newsletter.

For example, one of my target markets is coaches, so I offer 50 power questions that coaches can put to use immediately in their coaching practice (see additional resources at the end of the chapter).

If you're challenged in writing your "free download," or just want to save time, you could "borrow" a freebie from someone else. Start by searching for an article on your topic using Google. For example, you could Google, "newsletter article double your energy." Here's the process:

1. find an article you love
2. ask permission to give it away if it's not already clear in the fine print
3. add a link to the author's site
4. add a link to your site
5. add an ad for any product you might be promoting (if any)
6. convert the document into an Acrobat (.pdf) file so that people can view it no matter what software they have, and so they can't alter the document once you've "published" it (hint: you can use the free tool at www.cutepdf.com or see additional resources at the end of the chapter).

Now you have a valuable free download to offer.

DAY 2 — SET UP YOUR NEWSLETTER SYSTEM

Now that you have a captive audience, it's time to choose a newsletter service so you can send it. This is an online service that manages your subscription database and sends out your newsletter for you. Why not just use Outlook or Apple Mail or Gmail? Because an online service can:

- Send thousands of emails at a time
- Send an automated sequence of emails (autoresponders)
- Allow people to unsubscribe by clicking one link and
- Increase the chances of your email bypassing the Gmail and AOL spam filters, due to the provider's good reputation

A Cool Package

The system I've used for eight years now to build my business is Professional Cart Solutions (a private label of the better known

1 Shopping Cart). For a start it has your newsletter system and shopping cart system — the web page that takes customer orders — all integrated in one package. It also has affiliate management software built in, which will become important down the track when you're ready to have an army of people selling your products for you (and all set on automatic). It has advanced tools to track the performance of your ads and email campaigns to see what's working, and when you're ready to accept credit cards they can also set up your merchant account to accept money.

I like this kind of all-in-one package because everything is in the one place, and for less than $50 a month. You don't need to select three different systems and try to get them to talk to each other. If you get stuck you can use their online support, call upon your Web Wizard if you've chosen to hire one, or hire one of the Virtual Assistants they recommend. For more on this option see www.GetPaidForWhoYouAre.com/pcs.

Another cool yet significantly more expensive option is InfusionSoft. When you have over $50,000 in sales this becomes a good option (see additional resources at the end of the chapter).

The Shoestring Budget Alternative

If your bank account is running on empty and you can't afford the $25-$50 per month for Professional Cart Solutions, there is another option — www.MailChimp.com is free until you hit 500 subscribers and packed with powerful features. It just may take a bit more time to integrate with a separate shopping cart, and when you have to start paying you might decide to switch to Professional Cart Solutions anyway. Other well known services include www.aweber.com, www.constantcontact.com, and www.icontact.com.

With www.GoWeeblyNow.com for your website, www.MailChimp.com for your newsletter and autoresponder software and www.PayPal.com for your shopping cart (discussed in Chapter 6 when we talk about product) you can have a nice little ecommerce system for free, or very close to free.

DAY 3 - PUT A SIGNUP FORM ON YOUR WEBSITE

Once you've created a free download, you'll need to create a web form so that people can sign up for it. You can put this on your home page. I also suggest you put a signup form on every single page in the same location, at the top left or top right of the page.

You're leading with the free download as the main draw, but you also want people to subscribe to your newsletter. Here's an example of how to do it, taken from my site at www.solutionbox.com/freedownload.htm:

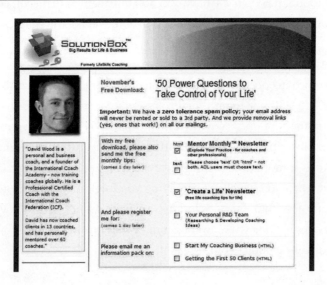

"Should I charge for my newsletter?" Freedom Ninja says: Probably not. The purpose of your newsletter is to build trust and relationships with customers and bring them into your "product funnel" (see below). Later on, you'll have plenty of chances to convert newsletter subscribers into paying customers through premium membership sites and other products and services.

Download – FREE
Newsletter – FREE
CD – $27
CD Set – $197
DVD Program $497
Services $500-2000 Per Month

What to expect

Coming up with material to put in your newsletter can take as little as 20 to 30 minutes an article. If you send out two articles a month, you're committing to one or two hours a month, assuming you've set up your newsletter system. Setting up the initial system, which includes creating your subscription page, converting your current contacts into newsletter subscribers and setting up a newsletter template, will probably take a total of 10 to 15 hours.

DAY 4 - CONVERT YOUR CURRENT CONTACTS TO SUBSCRIBERS

You have an existing list of friends and perhaps colleagues, yes? Why not invite them to firstly advise you on what your newsletter should contain and secondly subscribe? See additional resources at the end of the chapter for more on this.

DAY 5 - CHOOSE YOUR NEWSLETTER DESIGN (TEMPLATE)

Should you send your newsletter in plain text or HTML? HTML emails allow you to add bold text, colors and graphics. I suggest you keep it simple and start with plain-text emails.

Freedom Ninja says: If you have your heart set on a colorful newsletter and want to invest a little extra time in creating an HTML newsletter now, the easiest way is to download a free or paid HTML newsletter template from the internet and then customize it to include anything that will appear in every newsletter, like your newsletter's name, your photo and a brief bio. Even better, have your Web Wizard design a template that matches your website so you are sending a consistent brand message. If you're using a template through a newsletter service like MailChimp, you can choose a template and easily customize it.

They are more likely to get past your subscribers' spam filters and reach their inbox.

You won't want to create your whole newsletter from scratch every time and you'll want a consistent look and feel for each one, the same way you want the pages of your website to be consistent. The best way to do this is to download a free or paid template from the web. You can find templates in both text and HTML versions by searching Google for "free newsletter templates". Or you're welcome to use mine — see additional resources at the end of the chapter.

DAY 6 — WRITE YOUR FIRST ISSUE!

Once you have your newsletter machine in place, it's time to fill it with good reading for your subscribers. There are many ways to do this and not all of them require you to write. Here are a few options:

- Write the article yourself
- Republish articles from other experts
- Hire a writer
- Buy articles

You can hire a writer through www.elance.com. To buy articles, check out www.Ready2GoArticles.com. If you use the code "solutionbox" when you're buying articles, you'll get 10 percent off.

For more detailed advice on how to easily produce newsletter content, see the "How to Easily Produce Newsletters" Guide at www.GetPaidForWhoYouAre.com/access.

> **"How long should my newsletter be?"**
> Not long. Once in a while I'll write a "long" newsletter of maybe seven or eight paragraphs, but I recommend you stick to two to three paragraphs. You know how busy you are and you know how busy your subscribers are, so two to three paragraphs should suit you both.
>
> **"How often do I send out a newsletter?"**
> I suggest every two weeks. If it's once a month or longer before people hear from you, they'll forget about you. If you publish twice a week, people are going to say, "Leave me alone!" Every two weeks is a good middle-ground.

DAY 7 - SEND IT OUT!

Once you've written at least one newsletter (though you could write more and "bank" them) it's time to send it out!

For now I suggest you simply write newsletters as you need them and click send so they are going out in "real time". You'll do this using the service you chose above on "Day 2".

ALMOST HALF-WAY THERE

Remember Marissa, who at the beginning of the chapter was trying to sell her bookkeeping service without a newsletter? Well, she finally got hip and decided to create a newsletter with up to date information to draw people to her website. Information was everywhere, so all she had to do was gather and organize the latest tips and advice for keeping business books in order. Once she had a couple of issues ready, she announced her newsletter and watched as the initial subscriptions rolled in. After a couple of months she had two hundred subscribers, began to get calls and referrals requesting a free consultation and landed two full-paying clients.

Make sure you've scheduled time to complete the action steps above — it's important. And, commit to these steps and set a deadline for completion with your Freedom Buddy.

With your newsletter system up and running, you'll be almost half-way to the finish line and well on your way to internet success! You'll have built the foundation of your empire through your website and newsletter system and you'll already be giving value to your growing list of customers. In addition, you'll be more "public" about what you're up to and may just find that people want to help you go further in getting paid for who you are.

Now, are you ready to create your very own product so you can impact people's lives and generate passive revenue?

Freedom Ninja Tip: Later on when you have more time, you can write say 20 ahead of time and queue them up as an automated sequence of emails (autoresponder). Then when people subscribe to your newsletter, they'll get say 20 issues over the next 10 months, without you lifting a finger.

RESOURCES

- Example of a dedicated newsletter page leading with a free download offer, taken from my site at www.solutionbox.com/freedownload.htm
- For a low cost, easy-to-set-up assessment or quiz to put on your site, visit www.GetPaidForWhoYouAre.com/assessments
- Free pdf conversion tool at www.cutepdf.com
- If you're not sure who to contact in your niche to find articles to republish, you could go to www.ideamarketers.com or www.ezinearticles.com and search hundreds of articles by category
- At www.Ready2GoArticles.com, if you use the code "solution box" when you're buying articles, you'll get 10 percent off
- For an online newsletter system: www.MailChimp.com, www.icontact.com, www.aweber.com, www.constantcontact.com
- **Get Paid University**
  (www.GetPaidForWhoYouAre.com/access)
  - "Freebie in a Flash" form, which will guide you quickly through creating your own freebie
  - "Friends Into Subscribers" Scripts for sample text you can send to your existing network to invite them to subscribe
  - Newsletter Templates, including the text template I started with
  - "How to Easily Produce Newsletters" Guide
  - 10 Newsletters In A Flash Worksheet to create 10 quick newsletters
  - "Create Your Newsletter" Expansion Module for further tips and strategies

Chapter 6

STEP 4: CREATE YOUR OWN PRODUCT IN **SEVEN DAYS**

Nancy Guberti, as a mother of a child with severe allergies, gained first-hand experience with many specialized diets, such as Wheat-Free, Gluten-Free, Dairy Free, Yeast-Free, Low Phenol Diet, natural detoxification protocols and supplement regimens. All she learned led to a passion to educate and empower parents with children that have been diagnosed with biomedical disorders. Now she is a certified holistic nutritionist and healthy lifestyle coach who has an internet-based business, with her own products. She is in business for real, just as you can be.

When you visit her website (www.coachforhealthyliving.com) just click on products and you'll see that as well as offering products from other experts, she has her own audio CD on "12 Steps to Promote a Healthy Lifestyle," which she sells for $24.99.

She initially launched this product to her email list and also offers it when she speaks publicly to various groups. So far she has received "amazing testimonials," she says, "on the difference this knowledge is making in the lives of others." She says, "I actually ended up getting more private clients as well after they purchased the audio CD", and referrals have also boosted her business.

She got started the same way you can. She made "To Do Lists, and dedicated specific days and blocks of time to get everything accomplished." She loves what she does, improves lives and is building a solid income.

This could be you I'm talking about.

Freedom Ninja says: Whether you're selling a product or a service, you need to offer an information product under $50.

Think about everything you know in your area of expertise. Your useful knowledge could range from building robots to weaving baskets, from horseback riding to nurturing plants. Now think about how many areas of expertise you have. Your interests may overlap into both travel and cooking international dishes. Further — think about all the life experience you've accumulated! For example, you may have hiked in every

National Park. This holds for transformational helpers, exotic pet owners, grandmothers connecting with grandkids, chiropractors and homeowners. You will see that you are a walking, talking storage place of information. What is that information worth to people who need it — $40? $5,000? Priceless?

How can you "clone" yourself to help an enormous number of people acquire this information 24 hours a day, seven days a week — and get paid for it?

The secret is to create informational, educational products and sell them on your website. Products enable you to have passive income — to make money even while you are asleep or on vacation.

WHY YOU NEED A PRODUCT

If you want to earn passive income, free up your time and serve more people, you absolutely *must* have a product to sell. I'll focus on information products because the profit margins are so high, because they cost close to nothing to produce. But the principles apply to any product.

Let's take a look at why product is so important to your online business:

1. Serve more people

Instead of serving, say, 20 people face to face, you can serve tens of thousands through your products.

For example, when I was group coaching or leading seminars, I found myself saying the same things over and over again. I started to lose interest. I decided to write everything down in a product called "CoachStart Manual," which teaches everything a coach needs to know to launch their business.

The CoachStart Manual (www.CoachStart.com) has now sold more than 6,000 copies in 52 countries.

By creating an information product, I automated my service to the world.

2. Paid auditions

When people buy your product, they are paying you to audition for them. Suppose you have a consulting or other service you'd like to sell to your web visitors. For example, if you're a dentist and a site visitor is thinking of switching to your practice, how will you help them make that decision? Many businesses rely on special offers and hope. But in our example, if the site visitor buys your CD explaining the Top Ten Tips for Oral Hygiene, it's like they are paying you to audition for them.

3. Be the expert

Have you noticed how when you know someone has written a book you assume they are an expert on that topic? As we read the book, assuming it's good, the perception strengthens. There's a similar effect when we listen to an MP3, read an ebook, or watch a video of someone. So in a way, creating a product on a topic positions you as an expert.

4. Self-expression

Take a look, if you get a moment to do so, at the website of Cheryne (Rocky) Brivik of Australia, who has — surprise, surprise — an internet-based business (www.contagious enthusiasm.com.au). Among the more than a dozen products she offers, one is a book: Be Enthused. It's a daily tool designed to get you heart-centered, into a place where anything is possible (in your case, perhaps starting your own internet-based business). The book is also offered in various forms, visual and audio. Now how cool must Rocky feel when she sees her name in print and knows she's helping others? Now, take a deep breath. Picture yourself in that position. What is it *you* most want to express to the world?

5. Personal satisfaction

One of the most rewarding aspects of creating your own products is people telling you how much it means to them. Recently, when I was at Harbin Hot Springs in Middletown, California, a man approached me.

"Are you Solution Box?" he asked.

"Well, that's my company, yes" I said.

The guy was really excited: "Man, I got the first speech that you ever did — "First 50 Clients" on CD - and it really inspired me. I've been using that to build my practice. It's awesome. Thank you so much."

I've also had people write and tell me my relationship ebooks (See www.TruthAboutWomen.net) changed their life. It feels so good to hear from people whose lives have shifted for the better because of your product.

6. Move customers through your product funnel

Finally, the big picture reason to have a product is to help move your customers through your Product Funnel (see Figure 6.1). Remember "flowers before sex in the Bahamas"? You don't try to sell someone your professional service, such as coaching or even dental work, up front. You cannot expect people visiting your website for the first time to make a significant purchase, because they don't even know you. That first meeting, just as in a social setting, comes off best when it is a low-pressure opportunity to be introduced and bond.

In order for people to buy from you, they must first like and trust you. You achieve that by doing what's called "relationship marketing" — building a relationship with your customer. You start by giving away a freebie such as a newsletter or a special report. In return, they give you their name and email address; they are now in your marketing "funnel." As people read your newsletters and get to know you, they may start buying small products, then bigger and bigger products.

Figure 6.1 — Your Marketing Funnel — Note that the prices are not set in stone, but are just examples. I'll often end a price in the number 7 because people seem to respond to that better. For your first product, you want to start with something simple and less than $50. Your goal is to turn your visitors into subscribers, and your subscribers into customers.

The funnel begins wide at the top, because many people will accept the freebie. Some of them may become customers and buy your CD.

As the prices get higher, smaller numbers of people will buy. But you need to create a wide funnel of potential customers to find the few who will eventually buy the high-price items. Remember, this is all done automatically, without you even being there.

Here's an example: Your potential customer Sue visits your website, which features one of your products. You "talk" to her through the text on the page and the audio message below your photo. She sees the "Free Report" and clicks the button. To receive the download, she supplies her name and email address.

Your system then emails her the free report and follows up with the free newsletters she agreed to receive. After three weeks, she may have read up to six messages from you.

After reading your newsletters for three weeks, Sue might click on a link that takes her back to your website to buy a product. As soon as her credit card is processed by the system you have set up, an email automatically appears in her inbox containing the download link — costing you nothing for paper, shipping or production. You have set it up so that everything happens automatically. You can collect money in your PayPal account without even being online.

So, you need to have a product to help your customers move through your Product Funnel, to buy your next product or professional service, further down the funnel.

NEED A CONFIDENCE BOOSTER?

Sometimes when I create a new product I think "Hang on, who am I to position myself as an expert and offer advice?" If this resonates with you, see Section A in the bonus materials at the end of the book, particularly the heading "Can I really make a difference?"

WHAT TO EXPECT

It might take three or even seven products before you find one that really takes off. I'll tell you how to do the research so that you pick a product that's more likely to be a winner from the start. Expect a significant learning curve. It's unlikely that you will pick a hit product right away. You need to be persistent, knowing that you're training yourself in how to create and sell successful products. In fact, if your first three products only make back their costs and you get to build an initial list of customers, it's still a big win.

TYPES OF PRODUCTS

Let's brainstorm some ideas for your first product.

You can put your content into a printed book, report, manual or PDF file. I don't generally recommend you create an ebook. They sell for about $27 at most, and many people don't want to wade through as many as 100 pages for the information. Printed books are even worse — they take an enormous amount of time to write and sell for $15.95. And if you go with a publisher you normally only get 7% of that!

But if you name something a "Special Report," consumers tend to respond better, because there's a higher perceived value. The report might only be four pages or twenty pages.

But because it's a summary, people can just get the information they need. The $7-$47 they spent seems worthwhile.

People also perceive audio as having higher value. For example, a book might sell for $15.95, but the audio version might sell for $29.95. You can sell your information as a downloadable MP3 file or a CD. And if you start including video the perceived value keeps climbing.

Here are some formats you can use to create downloadable "virtual" products:

- Special report or article
- ebook (eworkbook, ejournal, emanual)
- Online assessment or quiz
- Paid ezine (internet magazine) subscription
- Members-only Website (or blog, forum or discussion board)
- MP3 audio file (for download or streaming)
- Interview or teleclass transcripts (pdf format)
- Online video
- ecourse (series of emails or online lessons, perhaps combined with audio and video)
- Access details for a teleclass, live or recorded
- Telecourse (series of teleclasses, live or recorded)
- Webinar (web-based seminar with audio and video)

Here are some formats for tangible products to ship:

- Printed book (booklet, workbook, manual, journal)
- Magazine or newsletter subscription
- CD or CD set
- DVD
- CD-ROM (data a computer can read)

You can also create a combination of all of the above. But don't feel overwhelmed by the choices. In a minute I'm going to make it really simple for you.

PRODUCT AT THE SPEED OF SOUND

I recommend you start with audio. Using audio, you can "create products at the speed of sound" as my good friend and internet marketer Alex Mandossian likes to say. Imagine you're on a conference call with a few friends discussing a topic you're passionate about. You record the call, giving you your first MP3 product. You then have that transcribed and you have a bonus written product to go with it. If it turns out to be popular you could have a CD manufactured and now you have a combination of an MP3, transcription, and physical CD — all from 60 minutes talking with your friends!

Freedom Ninja says: Write the sales page before you create the product. As you write, you'll be stating the benefits of this product and putting yourself in the customer's shoes. You may also start to feel excited about the product. You'll start to get a sense of what the product needs to look like, and perhaps think of bonuses you can offer with the product to sweeten the pot.

HOW TO PICK WHAT'S HOT

Let's say your niche is gardening, and you want to help people to be better gardeners. You can ask everyone you know:

"What do you love most about gardening?"

"What frustrates you?"

"What are challenges you have overcome?"

"What do you want to know about gardening?"

"What kind of gardening products have you bought recently?"

"What kind of training materials have you bought?"

"What advice would you give to someone getting started in gardening?"

Freedom Ninja says: Down the track when you are ready to get more advanced, you might create a membership site which people will pay you a monthly fee to access. You might add worksheets, special reports, audio, video, and a discussion forum so your members can support each other. One example is www. GetPaidForWhoYouAre.com/access which I created to support readers of this book. For inexpensive software to run this, try www.Wordpress.com combined with a program called Wishlist Member. For a high end option, visit www.GoMemberGate.com.

The answers you hear can spark some ideas about the type of product you want to create and the content you might put in it.

Reading magazines in your niche will also tell you the trends. Suppose you help women with relationship issues. You can get a copy of *Cosmopolitan* to see what's hot, what's selling. You might not find specific information products, but it will give you ideas. Is there an article about how to deal with relationship break-ups, or how to get attention from your man? That's what women are paying money to learn about.

HOW TO CREATE A PRODUCT IN SEVEN DAYS

While I call this section: "How to create a product in seven days," you can really do this in seven hours! It's that hot.

Here are the magic seven steps:

1. Pick a topic.
2. Schedule a teleclass. (Go to www.freeconferencecalling.com for their free teleconferencing service).
3. Book five friends, clients or colleagues to attend the call.
4. Beforehand, ask them to give you their top five questions about the topic.
5. Based on those questions, come up with a rough outline for the call (just pick the best questions).
6. Hold a 60 minute teleclass
7. Download the recording from the teleconference website.

This recording is your product which you can now sell as an MP3 file available for download! If you did a good job in the teleclass, you won't even need to edit the file.

Freedom Ninja says: If you want to get fancy... here are some optional steps if you have the extra time and energy. If you go a little further in refining your product you can increase the product price, or just be rewarded by the joy of adding value.

Do 4-5 versions of the same teleclass. Each time you will refine and improve it. Then choose the best recording and that's your product. Create an edited version of your audio file. You can find someone on www.elance.com to add music at the beginning and end and take out any irrelevant sections like the 5 minutes where you are waiting for people to join the call. This should cost you under $100.

Create a transcript. Again, go to www.elance.com and find someone to turn one hour of audio into a polished transcript for $50 to $150. For bonus points, have them do a little editing to take out the ummms and errrrs and have it read a little smoother.

Create a special report. Take that transcript and turn it into a report. Hire an editor to pull out the top seven points, create headlines and sections and format it nicely. You've now got a two- to four-page report.

Create a product. Have you noticed how even when you're buying a digital download, the sales page shows a nice 3D box with a big headline and a smiling person on it? That's because it looks more tangible, like something you could hold in your hands, and sells better. Ask a graphic designer on www.elance.com for a 3D box to represent your product for under $100.

Create a physical CD. Have your new graphic designer tweak the 3D box cover into a flat 2D CD cover. You can sell your CDs from the website, or at your speaking events if you decide to speak to promote your business.

HOW TO CREATE YOUR TELECLASS OUTLINE

Asking your teleclass participants what they want to know (Step 4 above) is just one way of creating your teleclass outline. You can also go to www.Amazon.com and find books on your topic. If the Table of Contents is available online, scan through it to get further ideas for your teleclass. A simple Google search on your topic will also generate a lot of articles you can quickly scan. How do you think I got the outline for this chapter?

Let me show you how easy it can be. One of my newsletter subscribers wanted to do a teleclass on conflict resolution. We were able to brainstorm a sample outline in less than five minutes:

- Types of conflict
- The damage caused by unresolved conflicts
- The benefits of resolving conflict quickly
- The power of curiosity in conflict resolution
- Case studies
- Technique: Listening and repeating
- Five power questions to ask in conflict
- Further resources

There's your outline!

TELECONFERENCE SERVICES

You can get free teleconference phone services, which I've been using for years. The free ones will typically take up to 100 people. Look for one that allows you to record the call and download it afterward. Also, test out the bridge to make sure you are happy with the reception quality and that people are easily able to join and are not kicked off the call. Fancier bridges allow you to log in online, see all the callers and see who has pressed a button to ask a question. Check out www.FreeConferenceCalling.com, www.InstantConference.com and www.FreeConference.com.

If you'd like a higher end solution, you can try the service I'm about to switch to, www.MyInstantTeleseminar.com. This service allows your attendees to use the old fashioned phone, or up to 2000 people can listen along via the web. When you're done, it makes the call available for instant replay for those who missed it — plus some other ninja features such as collecting participant questions prior to the call. At the time of writing they were offering a $1 trial for 21 days.

HOW TO SET THE PRICE

If you are creating an MP3, find out what similar MP3s, CDs or live teleclasses are selling for. You might even buy one to see what they provide.

You can also give your product to a few friends and colleagues and ask what they would expect to pay for it.

Another thing that affects price is the nature of the information. If your topic is "How to Have a Good Relationship" you can't charge as much as "How to Make a Million Dollars Flipping Real Estate". If it's a hot relationship CD, maybe it's $17 to $27 and you'll probably have to load it with bonuses. If it's about investing in real estate, you can get away with more — say $47.

TOOLS TO SELL THE PRODUCT

You need a few systems set up to sell the product. These include:

- Sales page
- Merchant account
- Shopping cart
- Drop shipper

Freedom Ninja says: To be realistic, it can take a good three months or even longer for you to climb the learning curve and become comfortable in all four of these areas. Hiring a Web Wizard who is familiar with the shopping cart you decide to use will accelerate the process enormously, so I highly recommend this. The beauty of it is, once you've done it all for your first product, the second one is a piece of cake. That's when serious revenue becomes more realistic.

SALES PAGE

You don't need to know how to create a sales page (the page on your website that sells your product) because you can find someone to do it for you. Go to www.elance.com and post a job request for a 500-word sales page to sell your product. Say that

HTML skills are required so they can create the actual web page and ask for work samples and a price quote. Then watch the bids come in, review their samples and see how well they are selling themselves. A reasonable price would range from $200 to $1,000, depending on how much you can afford. For an example of a sales page that I wrote in about a week, see www.FirstFiftyClients.com

MERCHANT ACCOUNT

A merchant account is a business account that allows you to collect payments from your customers' credit cards and bank accounts. You can sign up for an account through providers such as Secure Pay, www.2CheckOut.com or Practice Pay Solutions. I like Practice Pay (www.GetPaidForWhoYouAre.com/pps) because they are the sister company to Professional Cart Solutions, the shopping cart and newsletter system I recommended in Chapter 5, so they can talk to each other if any problems come up. At least in the beginning, don't bother with checks or cash. Only take credit cards.

PayPal and Google Checkout are alternatives to getting a merchant account. They are great for newbies entering the market, because you can set up an account in minutes, there is no setup fee, the charges are reasonable and you don't have to worry about a credit check. I recommend that to keep it simple you start with PayPal.

However, when you reach more than $30,000 a year in sales, it might be time to upgrade to a standard merchant account. You get your money more quickly, it's FDIC insured and you can customize more features.

YOUR SHOPPING CART

A shopping cart allows customers to enter their credit card details and buy your product. That information is then passed to the merchant account to verify that the funds are available. Once that is verified, the shopping cart can deliver a "Thank you" page to the customer, add the customer to its database and send a "thank you" email and further notices to buy the next product. They often come bundled with other magic things like autoresponders (automated sequences of emails sent over time), ad tracking and affiliate management software.

The two industry leaders are Professional Cart Solutions (a private label or franchise of 1 Shopping Cart) and Infusionsoft. I've used Professional Cart Solutions for years and can highly recommend it. Infusionsoft has more sophisticated customer follow-up technology, but is more expensive.

DROP SHIPPING

You do *not* need to produce a physical product yourself. And do *not* mail it to customers yourself. I did this with my "First Fifty Clients" CDs to save money. It was fine for the first 10 products, but it slowed me down too much after that. Fulfillment and drop shipping companies are so fast and inexpensive now, you have no excuse not to use them. You send them an MP3 and a graphic for the CD and the CD cover, which they might even help you create. They press the CDs, then ship them when the orders come in. They'll also handle returns.

I've been very happy with www.SprocketExpress.com in the U.S. and I know someone who has used www.Disk.com and had good results.

You might say, "But I could do it for free." No. That half-hour you take to fulfill an order is better spent creating more content and selling it.

Now that you have a sales page, merchant account, shopping cart and drop shipper, you're ready to sell your product!

HOW TO SELL YOUR PRODUCT!

The simplest way to sell your product is to place an ad on your website, in your newsletter and in your freebie download that you're using to capture email addresses.

When you've completed all Five Freedom Steps, there are many more promotional strategies you'll want to learn. One is leveraging affiliate programs, so you can have hundreds of people selling your product for you. Other strategies include running teleclasses, writing articles, publishing interviews, leveraging case studies and testimonials, selling from the back of the room at events and product reviews. For detailed promotional strategies see the "Product Promotion Strategies" Report listed in the resource section at the end of this chapter.

I recommend you keep things simple at first and wait to dive into such things until your machine or system is up and running and all Five Freedom Steps are complete.

WRAPPING UP

It's time to give yourself a huge pat on the back. You've just finished reading about a crucial step in creating your online machine to serve the world: creating your very own product. If you haven't already, talk to your Freedom Buddy to plan the time it will take to create your product, and then go do it.

RESOURCES

- For an easy way to get transcript made from audio, visit www.verbalink.com
- Teleconference services at www.FreeConferenceCalling.com
- www.InstantConference.com, and www.FreeConference.com Higher end teleconference service with $1 trial for 21 days: www.MyInstantTeleseminar.com
- Find an expert to interview at www.eHow.com
- Call Recorder for Skype to record your teleclasses or interviews, available from www.ecamm.com (Mac) or www.skyperec.com (PC)
- View leading shopping cart websites at www.GetPaidForWhoYouAre.com/pcs and www.GoInfusionSoft.com
- www.Disk.com and www.SprocketExpress.com — fulfillment companies
- To run a membership site, try a www.Wordpress.com blog combined with a program called Wishlist, found at http://member.wishlistproducts.com. For a high end ninja option, visit www.GoMemberGate.com.
- **Get Paid University** (www.GetPaidForWhoYouAre.com/access)
    - Sample four-week teleclass series structure
    - List of recommended credit card merchant accounts
    - "Product Promotion Strategies" Special Report

Chapter 7

STEP 5: GET **MASSIVE** TRAFFIC TO YOUR WEBSITE

It's never a surprise to Brian Johnson when he answers a ring at his door to find someone has sent him a free case of wine. Free! Did I mention free?

They do this because Brian's passion is tasting, comparing and reviewing wine and his website (www.thewinebloggers.com) is ranked as one of the very top on Google for "red wine reviews". Yet he still always gives a fair and honest review and the wine makers who send him the wine expect nothing less.

The not-so-secret secret of Brian's success is being willing to actually start. He says, "I tell a lot of people right now to get started and build some kind of momentum. Set up a Word Press blog (or Weebly site) even if all it has is your name at the top and just a couple of posts. This way you can get your feet wet and get some activity going. From there you can add features and build social media around that — once you have the foundation started." He says, "Actually, this is pretty easy, once you have the system set up. I just keep adding new content to keep things fresh. It's even easier when you invite guests to post."

A key issue is to stay targeted. Brian does wine, only wine. And there's always more wine to taste. Another key is not trying to work alone. Brian says, "You can also create joint ventures with websites that are starting with the same kind of niche. Don't look at them as competitors; look at them as friends. You should also realize this will take time — it isn't going to happen in a week or a month."

The proof is in the pudding, or in this case in wine. All you have to do is go to Google and type in "red wine review" and there will be his website, full of momentum and success, with him ready to hoist a glass in a toast to your success as well!

Freedom Ninja says: Don't expect results in a week. Building web traffic takes consistent work over several months. Are you willing to make mistakes and learn from them?

OUR JOURNEY THUS FAR...

When you have completed all the steps so far, you will have a core website that targets a very specific market that you care about and you'll be providing a valuable solution to those people visiting your site. You will have some information on your site, a free download in exchange for an email address and a newsletter with interesting information that builds a relationship with your customers over time.

You will have your very own product to sell, which makes a difference in people's lives, and can generate passive revenue for you. All you need now is for people to visit your website — preferably in droves!

Unless you know how to drive a lot of traffic to your website, it will remain one of the millions of un-findable could-have-been sites.

In this chapter I'll show you how to create a constant flow of targeted traffic to your site. I want you to know it takes time and persistence. But the results are well worth it.

SHIFTING YOUR THINKING

This is crucial: stop thinking about getting your website out there and start thinking about getting your compelling offer, such as a free download, out there. Would you best respond to "Visit my site at www.MySite.com", or "For a free 15 minute audio download on how to lose weight in 30 days, visit www.MySite.com"? If necessary, review Chapter 5 on creating your "freebie download" offer.

Throughout this chapter, instead of "list your website" I'll say "list your compelling offer".

Freedom Ninja Tip: If you're looking for one place to focus in this whole chapter — focus on writing articles (or having them written for you) under 'Search Engine Optimization' later in this chapter. Choose that method, or one other method that draws you such as social media or public speaking, and go deep with it. Don't try to do all the methods all at once. And go easy on yourself. You're getting a *lot* of information in this book, and it's OK if it doesn't all sink in at once — that's what re-reading is for. If it ever starts to look a little overwhelming, just remember how you eat an elephant: one bite at a time.

ONE TO ONE METHODS

No-brainer one to one methods (and by this I mean reaching one person at a time) include putting your compelling offer on a business card and handing it out to as many people as possible; putting it on your stationery; and putting it in your email signature, so that every email you send has the potential to draw the reader to your website.

Networking events are good places to hand out your business card, but two caveats:

1. Please ask people first if they would like one — I get so annoyed when people assume and thrust one in my face; and

2. It's much more important to get *their* card. That way you can follow up personally, find out what they need and if receiving your newsletter would be beneficial to them. Remember, you want to build a relationship with people over time and your newsletter is a great way to do it.

The advantage of the above methods is that they are simple and easy to do. However, to reach more people with less time, let's take a look at some more powerful methods.

PUBLIC SPEAKING

Public speaking is a great way to get new customers and newsletter subscribers, and drive traffic to your website. This is one of the early ways I built my business. Approach local clubs and/or businesses in your area and offer to come and speak for free. During your speech, and on any handouts, you can mention your compelling offer (i.e., your freebie download, as explained earlier).

PUBLICITY

Consider taking advantage of free publicity to get your website noticed. Let's say, for example, you notice something interesting in the news related to what you do. Call your local radio station or newspaper and say, "Hey, I see that this is happening in society right now. Would you like to do a story on that? I can provide some expert commentary". Or, "I just had a client switch careers inside 30 days, and I'm thinking this is part of a general trend." There's a good chance your website will get plugged. And of course, bonus ninja points if you get your compelling offer plugged.

As I mentioned earlier, choose one method in this chapter and go deep. If you're going to focus on publicity, it can be very rewarding. Study everything you can on the internet for free, and spend a solid 3-6 months on this.

SOCIAL MEDIA

Traditional media no longer have a monopoly on what we see or hear. With sites like www.Digg.com, readers themselves decide what is important and which stories float to the top. You can now have your very own TV or radio show and broadcast it online. In a way, your website, newsletter, Facebook profile

Freedom Ninja Tip: Rather than just hoping a speaking audience visits your website, here's a very powerful technique to collect their email addresses on the spot! In the last couple of minutes say "Feedback from you is how I improve. I'd like to take a couple of minutes to get your feedback now", and then you hand out a form, and *wait a minute while they fill it in*. This collects their comments, but also what they are interested in and their contact details! It's a brilliant way to get more speeches, more newsletter subscribers and more clients! Your leads will go up by a factor of ten. See the resources at the end of this chapter for the form I use.

or Twitter account is like having your own show, with your own audience.

Facebook allows you to create a personal or business profile, and then build your network of "friends". You can see what your "friends" are up to and they can see what you're up to. Facebook has over 300 million users and if it counted as a country would now be the 4th largest country on Earth. Twitter allows you to send a one-line update to people who are "following" you and to see the updates of people you are following. While Twitter only has 8 million members to date, it's currently growing at over 1,000% per year!

Let's look at the biggest networking tool, Facebook. You can't sell directly to people on Facebook because a culture is evolving where people expect useful content to be shared for free. Perhaps more than anywhere else, in social media you have to build a relationship first, build your visibility and sell later.

Here are five steps for success on Facebook:

1. Set up a free profile and a free Fan Page (by the way you're welcome to join my fan page — just search on Facebook for "Get Paid For Who You Are™").

2. Display your most interesting and useful work and characteristics on your profile and Fan Page. Perhaps a picture of you sky diving? Testimonial from a well-known business person?

3. Import your address book so Facebook can connect you with the people you already know (i.e., you have their email address).

4. Post useful and interesting things on your profile, every day. It could be a business article you found on CNN,

a Youtube video of a dog rescuing a child, a quote from marketer Seth Godin, or a picture of your family reunion.

5. Visit Facebook group pages related to your industry and post the above content, plus engaging questions to start discussions. Request to be friends with people you find interesting or related to your target market, such as the administrators and participants in relevant groups.

Freedom Ninja Tip: Instead of trying to sell to people on Facebook, focus on connecting with potential joint venture partners through Facebook! I'm currently Facebook friends with a Director at Virgin America and an Executive Vice President at AARP (a 40 million member organization). And they don't use their profile for business, as they only have about 80 friends each! I'm seeing family pictures, responding to personal posts and building a relationship. Wouldn't you rather set up a joint venture to offer your product to someone's 40,000 newsletter subscribers off-Facebook, rather than try and make friends with 40,000 Facebook profiles?

Once you have a certain critical mass (say 1,000) you'll find your network naturally grows as people see the useful and interesting content you're posting.

Every now and then let people know about your compelling offer and give them the link. This is how you transition people from Facebook watchers into newsletter subscribers, where you can build a deeper relationship and sell your products and services.

> Freedom Ninja Tip: Most people still aren't fully comfortable making videos. You can take advantage of this by posting an interesting or useful short video in relevant Facebook groups. At the end of the video you might even offer a free download for more information if they visit your website. Since people aren't posting a lot of videos, your video is likely to stay on the group's home page for several weeks.

Before we finish with social media let's quickly cover blogging. When you set up your website in seven days (Chapter 4) it's very easy to add a blog to your website, or in fact your entire site can be a blog. This invites interaction as people can post their comments and often link back to useful blog posts. Search engines like blogs because they have continually updated content.

You can generate visibility for your website by subscribing to the top 20 blogs in your industry, regularly commenting on posts you find interesting and including a link to your website at the bottom. Note: Most blogs are set up so that Google won't follow the links and give importance or Page Rank credit to your site, but people will see you, your link, and may visit your site.

Reminder: if you're going to focus on social media, spend 3-6 months just on that, and go deep. Don't just dabble in this and 2-3 other methods, or you'll get scattered and likely fail to produce traffic.

SEARCH ENGINE OPTIMIZATION (SEO)

Search engine optimization is really a technical way of saying: How do I get to the top 10 on Google? SEO, by the way, is one of the buzz acronyms, so once you have it under your belt you are officially "hip".

For me, this has been the most important tool to get web traffic and visibility within my industry. If you're slightly technically-minded you can do this yourself. If you're not, you can hand this chapter to your Web Wizard (if you chose in Chapter 4 to hire one) and get some help. With six months of consistent work, you can have a steady stream of free traffic. Let's cover a brief overview of the process here, and then you can turn to the back of the book when you're ready to roll up your sleeves and really jump into the details.

Here are the three most important steps:

1) Pick your keywords
The words a person is searching for on Google are sometimes called "keywords". For example, if you're a chiropractor in

Dallas, you're interested in people searching for the keywords "chiropractor Dallas". With a little research you can come up with a list of the main words your potential customers are using to try to find you.

2) Create your web pages

Once you've chosen your keywords, you'll create an article or page based on each keyword or keyphrase, e.g. "chiropractor Dallas", then ask your Web Wizard to make sure that the keywords appear in all the right places on the page for Google to like it. This increases your chances of Google serving you up in the top ten listings when people enter your keywords into a search engine.

3) Get links to your site

You can have the best content in the world, but if no one's linking to you, Google won't believe you. You have to have other websites link to you to be credible with Google — say about 30-50 links. One great way to do this is to write useful articles (revolving around specific keywords or key phrases) and post them on article sites around the web, with a link pointing back to your site.

Freedom Ninja says: When you're ready to roll up your sleeves and jump into how to implement these steps, turn to Section D in the Bonus Materials in the back of the book.

PAY PER CLICK ADVERTISING (A COMMENT)

You should also be aware of another traffic-generating strategy called Pay-per-click (PPC) advertising. I decided not to cover PPC in this book because it can be expensive, is far more competitive than when it first came out, and it can be quite overwhelming to learn when you have so many other things on your plate. I'd prefer for someone starting out — unless you're quite technically minded — that you focus on one of the other methods in this chapter.

That being said, if you focus your campaign, invest a lot of time and effort and follow the right strategies, you can still generate a lot of sales and leads using PPC. For training in this area see the "Pay Per Click Advertising Strategies" Report listed in the resource section at the end of this chapter. For strategies on how to capture your visitor's email address and how you can sell products to make back your advertising costs, check out the Online Bonus Chapter: Building a Massive Email List, listed in the same section.

BUILD OVER TIME

It takes time to attract traffic to your site. Be willing to go deep into one (two at the most) of the above traffic methods and explore to see which works best for you. If you're getting 2,000 visitors a month to your website after 6 months of effort, I'd call that a win.

Set up with your Freedom Buddy a consistent traffic building schedule. For example, you might dedicate five hours a week to building traffic. Perhaps you'll focus on building your Facebook following, or exchanging links with other websites.

You might write five articles a week, put them up as web pages, and then post them in ezine directories. Or perhaps you'll choose public speaking or publicity as your main strategy and book gigs or interviews.

You will have the peace of mind that comes from knowing you have set up a machine that will serve others and yourself for many years to come. It will take some tender love and care to tweak and build the machine to where you want it to be. This mainly involves testing and adjusting your offers until they are selling really well, and building, building, building your traffic streams.

But, at the end of this step, you will have built the critical structure for success in a fraction of the time it can take most people.

RESOURCES

- See Section D in the back of the book, for a more detailed description of the Search Engine Optimization (SEO) Process
- For training on how to get started as a public speaker, see my CoachStart Manual available at www.CoachStart.com
- Post on Facebook and Twitter at the same time using www.TweetDeck.com
- For great keyword ideas, go to Google's keyword tool at https://adwords.google.com/select/KeywordToolExternal
- To learn about Pay Per Click Advertising on Google, see www.google.com/adwords/learningcenter/
- A free online site/course to help you rank top ten with Google can be found at www.buildwebsite4u.com

- For help with building links to your website, see www. LinksManager.com
- For an SEO expert to optimize your website and increase your rankings, go to www.elance.com or www.rentacoder.com
- **Get Paid University** (www.GetPaidForWhoYouAre.com/access)
  - Expansion Module: "How to Get Massive Traffic" — for more on getting traffic
  - "Pay Per Click Advertising Strategies" Report
  - Online Bonus Chapter: "Building a Massive Email List" - for even more advanced methods of getting traffic and building your email list
  - Speaker Feedback Form — a ninja form I use to collect leads and email subscribers at a speech
  - Extended interview with Brian Johnson, wine blogger

Chapter 8

HOW TO GIVE **AND** GROW YOUR BUSINESS

It was 7 a.m. on a Friday. I woke up, felt my face and it was wet. I realized I was weeping.

Six months earlier I had attended a seminar in the Napa Valley and saw Brendon Burchard get up and speak. Off stage I'd thought he was kind of boring. But as he continued to speak from the stage something stirred inside me. By the end of his 90 minutes, I was so moved by the potential of partnering with nonprofits — that I was ready to don a robe, drop everything and follow him. I felt excited enough to later attend a training session he gave to learn exactly how to do it.

The tears came, on the second morning of the training, when I suddenly saw the possibility of making a really big impact in the world through supporting nonprofits, *and* growing my business at the same time.

It had been a huge conflict for me and I didn't even know it. I had spent years growing my business because I wanted financial security and abundance. I wanted to help charities and nonprofits and always thought I would do it — some day. But I was convinced it was an either/or situation — I could either work my business or I could support a cause.

Brendon was showing me how to do both. I could support a cause and it wouldn't have to take time away from my business. In fact, supporting a cause could help me generate more sales, revenue, credibility and media publicity. That's when I got all misty. When I realized that I could do both, my working life took on a whole new meaning.

A TWO-WAY RELATIONSHIP

Typically, when people think of supporting a cause, they think of donating resources or volunteering time. Some companies let their staff spend half a day a week supporting any cause that they want on paid company time. That's exciting. And it's possible to go deeper. You can support a cause in a way that gets you more customers and revenue, by creating a two-way partnership rather than a one-way relationship.

AUTHENTIC GIVING

This approach requires a change in our thinking about nonprofit organizations and causes. Many of us have been taught to give discreetly and that it is noble to be an anonymous donor. Get ready to have those notions challenged. Not only can you give to a cause in a highly public way, but you can actually profit from it as well.

You might ask, "Is that inauthentic?" Inauthentic would be picking a charity you really don't care about and pretending you do. But picking a charity you care about and shouting about it to the world, that's authentic.

Giving discreetly — also known as "anonymous good" — is a beautiful thing. It feels good because you know it can't be for anything else other than to do something positive. No one knows about it but you. What I am suggesting is something you can do in addition to your anonymous giving. It's a symbiotic relationship that will support a cause and your business at the same time.

Instead of keeping quiet about it, tell everybody you know about the organization and invite your database to get on the bandwagon. Tell them, "This is how you can do it too. I'm supporting my favorite cause and you can support it too by buying a product (like my CD) or a service (like my lawn trimming service) and telling all of your friends."

WAYS YOU CAN HELP A CAUSE

Let's look at specific ways you can support a cause, from outright donations to working partnerships.

1) Donate your product or service

The most basic way to support a cause is to donate your product or service. This product or service can be given to staff members, volunteers, beneficiaries, or even board members. For example, if you're a coach, like me, it's pretty straightforward — you offer your coaching service. The staff members of nonprofit organizations are usually paid only modest salaries, so your coaching service could be a nice fringe benefit.

You might call a nonprofit organization's CEO and say, "I've been wanting to give to a cause that I'm really passionate about. I was thinking about how I could do that. I'm a coach and I would like to offer my coaching services. I'm thinking your staff might be more productive and happier, and you might retain them longer if they had a coach who could help them with their goals. If I work with them, I could pick one goal that's personal to them and also one that's related to their work."

If you were a CEO and someone offered you X hours of free coaching for your staff, do you think you would say yes?

Are you a financial planner, teacher, some kind of trainer, or even a masseuse? Do you have an interest or make a product that could be shared? Many different types of goods or services can be donated.

2) Offer your product or service as a prize

You can offer your product or service as a prize for a sweepstakes or competition. In fact, why not reach out to 10 to 20 local nonprofit organizations in this way and start building relationships. For example, an accountant might donate 10 free tax returns to a charity raffle or auction.

One of my newsletter subscribers, Howard Van Schaik, has offered his coaching services as a prize for several silent auction fund raisers. He managed to convert some of those clients to paying clients and retain them for several months.

One author gave all of his royalties on one of his books to Doctors Without Borders. A scrapbooker worked with interested patients at a hospital to fill otherwise empty hours. A personal finance advisor helped people at a rest home iron out tax issues. A knitting enthusiast gave small comfort blankets to every baby born in her town.

3) Offer your product or service as a premium

You can also offer your product or service as an incentive when people sign up to the nonprofit's mailing list. If you go to the Sierra Club's website at www.SierraClub.org, they often offer a free rucksack when you become a member. If you happen to produce rucksacks, backpacks, caps or T-shirts, you could go to groups like the Sierra Club and donate your product. In exchange, they could acknowledge your company on their website and much more, which we'll cover later in this chapter.

You could do the same with information or digital products. Offer a free update, report or audio file as an incentive for people to sign up as a member with the nonprofit organization. Even though you are giving it away for free, every person who signs up for their mailing list will see your business name on the report.

Freedom Ninja Tip: Say to the nonprofit organization, "Let me set up a membership drive with your Web person. We'll test it for a week and you may find that your subscription rate increases by 10 to 50 percent. Let's do this as a pilot, and if it doesn't work, we can stop it." Everyone loves a pilot or a trial, because there's no commitment.

4) Speak at their events

Is making public speaking appearances one of the things you can or will do? Many nonprofit organizations have conferences, training seminars and conventions. They need speakers to train, inspire, and entertain their members and donors. As Brendon Burchard says, "Who attends fundraisers — influential or non-influential people?" Speaking at fundraisers can put you in front of CEOs and other leaders who could hire you to speak, or buy your company's product or service.

5) Give a percentage of profits

You could also donate a percentage of your annual profits to a cause. Again, try to do this as a partnership and create an agreement for what they will do in return. You may wish to tell them what your profits were last year and your projected earnings in the next year.

You can also do the same for a specific event or launch. Instead of giving a percentage of overall profits, you give a percent of sales earned for a particular seminar or a product launch. You could say something like, "You know, I'm launching an ebook next month and I'd be happy to give you 50 percent of the sale price. That can be huge for some nonprofits.

Example: Mary approaches Mental Health America and says: "I'm going to launch a book and I'd like to use this as a tool to raise funds and awareness for your organization. I'd like to offer you a percentage of royalties of the book. More importantly, I'd like to give you a percentage of backend sales." Backend sales are products sold after the initial purchase — so Mary sells her book on the front end and any follow on sales such as a companion CD would be considered backend sales.

She asks them in return to send an email to their database encouraging people to buy the book.

Example: After Hurricane Katrina I wanted to help the survivors. I thought, "Well, I could donate $5,000, or I could give $5,000 of value to my customers and raise the money that way." So I created a special product sale and announced: "If you buy this in the next 72 hours, 100 percent of the proceeds will go to Hurricane Katrina survivors." We raised $5,000 that way because people were thinking, "I'd like to donate anyway and now I get for free this product that I've been thinking of buying".

6) Logo Exposure

You can also offer nonprofit organizations exposure for their logos. Tell them that you will put their logo on your website, business card or newsletter, with a call to donate. The logo will also link to their organization.

Freedom Ninja Tip: The really big nonprofit organizations won't let you use their logo unless you have a major deal with them. Some of them even require you to pay money up front. But smaller nonprofits are more likely to be receptive.

7) Invite your customers to donate

You could say to the nonprofit organization, "It's not just what I'm going to be donating, but I'll also be inviting my customers to donate."

You can do this by sending requests through your newsletter, or by adding a donation request on the thank you page your customers see after each purchase: "Would you like to donate an extra 10 dollars to the Red Cross?" You could put a link on your website, or in an email they receive two days after they buy, saying, "I really hope you are enjoying the ab-cruncher. By the way, I wanted to let you know about a cause I'm passionate about. If you have a little surplus in your life right now ..."

Freedom Ninja Tip: When visitors to your website sign up to your newsletter, you might even add a little check box that says, "Are you interested in giving to charity?" This way you can compile a separate list of interested people, and can avoid sending a lot of solicitations to people who are not interested.

8) Newsletter exposure

Offer to include occasional stories about them in your newsletter. You might write about an interesting event they are holding, or feature a case study of someone they have helped — just as a news item next to your feature article. And of course — add a request to donate to their cause.

9) Media exposure

You could issue press releases about what the nonprofit is up to and how local businesses are supporting local causes. You could agree to mention them in every radio, TV and print interview you do.

10) Microgiving call

Invite all your customers and newsletter subscribers to join on a conference call designed to raise money for charity. You might have a prominent member of the community or a local celebrity join you as co-host. Discuss an interesting topic, and every 10 minutes invite people to go to the website and donate. Of course if you want to be old-fashioned, you can also do something like this in person and offer to host physical fundraisers.

CREATE PARTNERSHIPS

Again, you could give all of these things as a one-way donation. You'll get to feel good and you may even generate good will and sales from it without the charity doing a thing in return. However, why not offer a partnership? Why not go to your favorite nonprofit and say, "I'd like to use my business as a tool to raise funds and awareness for you and support your cause." And then later in the conversation, "If it's easy for you, would you be willing to get the word out about my business?" Now it's more of a comprehensive package, and a two-way relationship. They are used to such partnerships and are creating them all the time.

"Does my product have to be relevant to their cause?" Freedom Ninja answers: Well, it's easier if your product is directly relevant. The American Cancer Society is more likely to say yes to a health-based product than to an info product that stops divorce. So you should be looking for nonprofits where there might be a connection between your product or service and their cause.

HOW A CAUSE CAN SUPPORT YOU

A nonprofit organization can in return lift your credibility. Mentioning on your website that a portion of proceeds goes to support the local RSPCA, for example, generates good will and trust. A nonprofit organization can also reach out to its members and supporters to help generate sales for you. Let's look at some specific ways they can easily help that won't cost them dollars:

1) Website and Newsletter

A nonprofit organization can feature you on its website and describe their partnership with you, with a link to your website.

It could put you in an electronic newsletter. Such an organization usually does not want to advertise you, but could share an article about what you're doing with them. It might even do a blatant pitch for your product or service if it gets a percentage of the sale.

2) Press releases

They could issue press releases. You could tweak the same article that you wrote for their website, newsletter, or print magazine, into a press release for them to distribute. Who's the media going to pay more attention to — a press release from you, or a press release from them?

3) Direct mail

They could give you exposure via direct mail. Suppose you are launching a CD and you'd like to use it as a fundraiser for them.

Freedom Ninja Tip: A nonprofit organization can introduce you to sponsors. Once you've built a relationship with the nonprofit organization, you can ask them to introduce you to corporations who could be potential sponsors. You might say to the nonprofit: "I'd like to take this to the next level and do some radio advertising that also mentions you. I'd like to get funding for it, so who are you already working with? If you'd like, I'd be happy to approach them. Or if you'd introduce me that would be great. I'll see if they have room in their budget to maybe allocate an extra $10,000 to $20,000 and we'll get you on the radio."

They could put an ad for the CD in their electronic newsletter and on the home page of their website. And they could mail out a little flier. Now, you wouldn't expect them to mail it to everybody just for you, but you could say, "With the next mailing you're going to do, let's include this little flier as a fund raiser for you." Now you're reaching one thousand, five thousand, ten thousand, twenty-five thousand people by direct mail and it's saved you years of building your own database. You don't have to build the credibility and relationships that the nonprofit has built. You may not even have to pay for the postage (although you could offer to do so as a gesture of goodwill).

BONUS MATERIALS

For more information covering how to choose your nonprofit, how to approach them, what to include in a proposal and partnering with corporations, see Section E in the Bonus Materials at the end of the book.

WRAPPING UP

You don't have to partner with nonprofit organizations. But if you choose to, you can go to sleep at night feeling good, knowing that you're raising money for causes you care about. You may find that giving to others returns abundance to your family and friends. And, it's fun to have partners.

As your customers appreciate you supporting a cause and the cause helps you to reach their supporter base, you might find your business is growing twice as fast as it would without such partnerships.

And maybe, just maybe, it's OK to receive as you give.

RESOURCES

- Book Launch Sponsorship Proposal: <u>www.</u> <u>GetPaidForWhoYouAre.com/access</u>
- Brendon Burchard's Partnership Seminar training: <u>www.GoPartnershipSeminar.com</u>
- <u>www.CharityNavigator.com</u>, for researching nonprofit partners

Chapter 9

CONCLUSION: GO THOU AND DO LIKEWISE

At this point you have everything you need, unless you also need a firm and friendly kick in the butt to get moving. I'm way over here, so you may need to get a friend or Freedom Buddy to help you with that. Or, you can join the continuing education program and I'll happily play that role. More about that in a minute.

Allow me to pack the entire book into a 30 second summary for you:

TRUE FREEDOM!

You know that the biggest prizes in the package are the four freedoms:

- **Location Freedom:** the ability to live or travel anywhere in the world, including the simple joy of working from home
- **Time Freedom:** being able to choose to work five days a week, or one

- **Financial Freedom:** not having to check the prices when you buy things that bring joy to you and those you love and not having to worry about money again
- **Inner Freedom:** which is the freedom to express yourself, and to share what you know and love with the world.

WHO YOU HELP

Chapter 3 and the exercises in Section B should help you narrow in on the group of people you'd most like to serve.

SET UP YOUR WEBSITE IN 7 DAYS

The next step is to get a rough draft of your website up and running using www.GoWeeblyNow.com, by hiring a Web Wizard, or ideally both!

SET UP YOUR NEWSLETTER IN 7 DAYS

By now you may be feeling how absolutely critical a newsletter is to building relationships with a group of people who will some day buy from you. And you know how to set up a working version in under a week!

CREATE YOUR OWN PRODUCT IN 7 DAYS

Whether you already sell products or services, or are just beginning, you now realize the fundamental importance of offering an information product for less than $50 (see Figure 9.1).

Figure 9.1 — Your Marketing Funnel
And, you know the ninja process for getting
a first version out to market super fast.

GET MASSIVE TRAFFIC

Once you have your target market, your
website, your newsletter and a simple product, there's only one
thing left: people to visit your site! You now have a range of
options for generating web traffic, from free search engine
traffic to social media to public speaking.

GIVE AND GROW

Finally, you may by now be entertaining the exciting notion
that building a relationship with a charity or nonprofit
organization doesn't just look good, feel good, and do good —
it's good for business too!

CONTINUING EDUCATION

You may at times get in your own way and entertain limiting
beliefs that can slow you down or hold you back. That's
why I've busted open the Four Myths, shown you how you
can take small steps and encouraged you to seek outside
help where needed. And there's something else. If you need
help, don't hesitate to call on me. I can always be reached at
david@getpaidforwhoyouare.com.

I've also created a support program for those who are
serious about creating a lifestyle of freedom and contribution.
In your own life, you may have noticed that continuing
support can be the difference between success and failure, so I

want you to have every advantage you can get. As a member of Get Paid University you can download forms, worksheets, expansion modules, audio recordings and bonus chapters to help you implement the Five Freedom Steps (see the full list of resources in Section F). And as an owner of this book, you qualify for a month's free trial. Just enter the code "freedom" at www.GetPaidForWhoYouAre.com/access.

GO THOU AND DO LIKEWISE

Now it's time for us to part, Grasshopper. But always remember that I'm around, available to you, and am cheering you on all the way. I wish you every success!

I encourage you to support the work of these charities making a difference in the world.

Visit their website and consider volunteering your time or donating money:

Rainforest Action Network (www.ran.org)

Byron Katie's 'The Work Foundation'
(www.theworkfoundationinc.org)

One Laptop Per Child (OLPC)
www.laptop.org

BONUS
MATERIALS

SECTION A
Your Confidence Booster

Even after reading Chapters 1 and 2, it's understandable if you still have uncertainty given the huge possibility before you. You could find yourself thinking, "Maybe I should wait, take more classes, or clean my house first". I face doubt every day, *particularly* while writing this book. Fear not, my friend, for this section will remind you of the strong foundation you're already working from.

FOUR FACTORS YOU ALREADY HAVE (OR CAN EASILY GET)

Experience. You might be surprised how much life experience you have, once you begin to take stock. If you grew up with a plumber, if you've read a lot about acupuncture, if you've been through a divorce, if you like to go fishing or build model planes, this experience will stand you in good stead as you begin to help others. You don't have to pretend to be a top expert in your field. By reading the best 2-3 books on your topic, getting a regular magazine or two, and prowling the internet you'll end up knowing more than 95% of the population in that area. And you can connect with others with similar interests or experience and bring in guest experts to provide content. This gives you credibility, as well as free training! Ongoing learning is an essential part of the process... and the fun!

Passion. If your experience is in an area that's boring to you, pick another subject, one you like. Whatever you do, don't waste your time on something that doesn't excite you. You may be able to squeeze a little money out of it, but just think of the difference you could make if you were driven by real passion! The one exception to this is if you want to pick an area that doesn't quite float your boat to be your main bread-winner, because your major love is just too hard to make money in.

Perseverance. Not every step of your journey will feel like a victory. There may come a time when one of your customers complains or your computer crashes. Or you try five things in a row and nothing works. You start to wonder, "Why am I doing this?" Can you work your way through the challenge? Perseverance will help you to stay in the game, turn the challenge into an opportunity and turn what you've learned into a stronger and better you.

Support. Do you push away support? Maybe you don't want people to know that you can't do everything or that you don't have all the answers. Who does? To succeed at this game, you'll need support. Think of "getting help" as a skill you can develop and think of a person who's good at getting help as someone who can look at his strengths and weaknesses and find people to fill in the gaps. By taking on a mentor, or getting a Web Wizard, or even eventually hiring an assistant to help you along the way, imagine how free you'll be to focus on doing what you love!

CAN I REALLY MAKE A DIFFERENCE?

Whether you're sharing your passion, hobby, skill, experience or widget with the world, in Chapter 6 you'll see how important it is to offer an information product that adds value to people's lives. It's natural to wonder if you have what it takes to really help people move forward. Consider these thoughts:

I've found that it takes only one good tip or supportive gesture to change someone's day, week, month, or year.

One way to help others is to simply hold out the possibility to someone that their life will improve.

You can show someone where you've fallen down in your life, that you're a real person like them and that other people have these problems, too.

You can show someone a strategy to get out of a hole that they're in, that you've been in.

You can give someone case studies of people you've researched. "Here's how other people did it; you're not alone".

You can interview an expert and bring that material to your market.

You can present the information in a way they haven't heard before. For example, with a serious issue like divorce you might offer the viewpoint that it's the next adventure. It's not the end of one's life; it's the beginning of a second life.

BUILDING YOUR CREDIBILITY

Many people ask: "What if I lack credibility?" Balderdash! It's only possible to lack credibility if you pretend to be something you're not. Regardless of how much or how little experience you have in your niche, the following tips can help you build your credibility in the eyes of others, and most importantly yourself:

Contribution. Is your attention on yourself, or on your customers? Focus on helping others: this will take the focus away from you and your fears and keep you steady.

Building knowledge. Build your knowledge and skills each day by reading, listening and even attending training for your niche. Knowledge is a big key to confidence and you'll gain a lot by learning all you can. In fact, read the top three books on your topic and you'll know more than 95% of the population in that area.

Mentorship. Find a mentor to help keep you on track with your goals. In addition, since your mentor will possess expertise in your niche, you will feel more confident knowing there is someone to go to with questions you can't answer.

Testimonials. Build results and get testimonials from your clients and even your friends. Not only do testimonials show the world you have something valuable to offer, they remind *you*.

Media. Call your local radio stations and newspapers to pitch an interview. You'll need to have a catchy angle that is more about a trend or issue related to your niche, rather than about you. This is a way for you to see that you have something to say that is of value to others. And with a couple of media mentions on your site, you'll look and feel like a professional. I like to put buttons on my site so people can listen to me being an 'expert' on radio. Think about it — as soon as one talk show host asks your opinion about something, you're an expert.

Interview Experts. If you interview five of the top people in your field, you'll pick up a lot of information that you can pass on to your clients. i.e., *you* are becoming the expert. You'll also have credibility by association with some big names and be forming invaluable relationships with the "big fish".

Partner with an expert. You can approach someone who's already made a name for himself or herself and is perhaps struggling with the web marketing, product creation and coordinating operations. Perhaps they'll groom you to build a reputation of your own.

Experience. If you're providing a service, get 50 clients under your belt. You'll not only start to feel like an expert, but from working with all their issues, you'll be one.

When I started coaching, I didn't feel I had "credibility." I invited my friends and colleagues to be "practice" clients and gave them a steep discount. When I had about 20 clients at one time, I started showing new coaches how to do what I'd done. After 12 months of that I became the coaches' coach and an "expert", ready to create new products. Do you see how it works?

You don't need to start with anything other than what you have — in fact that is the only place where you *can* start.

SECTION B
How to Find Your Perfect Niche —
More on Deciding WHO You Help

Now it's time for you to turn a corner in your career and join the ranks of passionate professionals who know exactly what they do and for whom — and who can communicate it clearly and powerfully in 30 seconds or less!

I'll give you five exercises to help you get clear on at least a possible group of people you'd like to help. Then, we'll boil it all down into one line.

Exercise 1: Take inventory
Let's start by taking inventory of the skills, knowledge and experience you have.

Freedom Ninja Tip: For the Take Inventory worksheet to help you with this section, go to: www.GetPaidForWhoYouAre.com/access and print it out.

Before you begin, make a cup of tea or pick up a latte and get comfortable. This is internal work, so find a quiet place where you can be free from distraction.

Next, look back over your life and work experience, including any volunteering you've done (nonprofits, churches, schools?) and other activities that are important to you. Make a list of them.

Which of these experiences did you *most* enjoy? Which most drew upon your core strengths? Who did you most enjoy working with? Who did you least enjoy working with? Who was a natural "fit" for you? Rank the top three experiences in a new list. For example, one of the best times of my life was being a camp counselor.

Next, take your top three and write down what type of work you were doing at the time. Here are some examples:

Teaching	Accounting
Human resources	Real estate
Public relations	Academic work
Marketing	Physical training or therapy
Engineering	Health and beauty
Business consulting	Construction
Interior design	Law
Landscaping	
Social work	

Then, next to each of these answers, note:

1. which strengths you used to do your job well; and
2. which helped to make it a satisfying experience.

For example:

Communicating	Influencing others
Organizing	Negotiating
Leading	Inspiring people
Managing	Writing
Getting things started	Analyzing
Follow through	Keeping people focused
Executing projects	Attention to detail
Designing	Developing procedures
Teaching or mentoring	Making things efficient
Learning	Anticipating problems or risk

Exercise 2: The problems you have fixed

Next, list what problems you have solved over your lifetime, both at work and with family and friends. These could be one-off problems, or problems that you have solved over and over. What challenges have you overcome? What problems have you solved for others? For example, I'm really good at helping people find the words for scary or difficult conversations. And I can help them find a name for their business that excites them. Here is a list of common problems that people and businesses face.

PERSONAL PROBLEMS

Stress	Not enough time
Lack of confidence	Can't set boundaries
Work pressure	Feeling unloved
Unhappy marriage or	Poor communication
relationship	Creative blocks
Addictions	Not enough money
Boredom	Obesity

Conflict at work

Isolation

Lack of work skills

Conflict at home

Disorganization

Negativity

Unemployment

Dependence

Grief

Illness

No routine

Poor social skills

No energy

Too much debt

Uncertainty

Phobias

Overwhelmed

Hate their job

No motivation

Procrastination

BUSINESS PROBLEMS

Poor sales

Ineffective marketing

No processes or consistency

Wasted time

Poor product or service quality

Poor customer service

High turnover rates

Employee conflict

Employees underperforming

Lack of teamwork

Low morale

Ineffective marketing

People burning out

Work/life conflicts

People feeling overwhelmed

Overspending or under-saving

Poor cash flow

Not enough income

Lack of forecasting

Poor communication

People stagnating in positions

Painful emotions

Negative feelings

Well, what did you discover?

These exercises will help you connect to what you have to offer. If for some reason it doesn't look like a lot to you, put that thought aside for a moment. Often we de-value what comes easily to us because it *is* so easy. However, in case you haven't noticed, it is *not* easy for others, which is why they will seek you out and pay you for it!

Exercise 3: Who do you want to help?

Now, let's brainstorm about who you would like to serve. And for this part of the process we're going to get a bit 'touchy feely'.

I want you to pay attention to how your body feels, because it will likely give you more honest guidance than your mind as to where your true passion is. For instance, you may *think* that it would be best for you to work with doctors because your mom always admired doctors. However, your body may feel hollow or tired at this thought and yet enlivened by the idea of working with acupuncturists. See if you can *feel* your way through the exercise.

Bring your awareness to your body and answer these questions:

Who would I love to work with?

What types of people have I most loved working with?

Who feels like a natural fit for me?

Who is intriguing to me?

Who most needs my help?

Who is not currently being helped enough?

Another way to approach this is to visualize working with people. As you sit in your quiet space, close your eyes and see yourself working with people in some of the groups you have identified. What are these people like? What do they have in common? Who *feels* the best to work with?

If you are still looking to identify a group or groups of people who "resonate" with you, here are a few ideas broken down by occupation, age, interest and marital status, to spark your brainstorming. See how you feel when you read each line. If anything sparks excitement or interest, circle them.

By Occupation

Entrepreneurs
Accountants
Doctors
Social workers
Managers
Virtual assistants
Teachers
Engineers
Architects

Coaches
Therapists
Executives
HR professionals
Salespeople
Marketers
Bankers
IT professionals

By Age

Babies
Toddlers
Preschoolers
School children
Pre-teens
Teenagers

Recent graduates
Twenty-somethings
Thirty-somethings
Middle-aged
Retired

By Interest

Animal lovers
Vegetarians
Artists
Train spotters
Surfers

Squash players
Computer techies
Wood workers
Quilters
Scrapbookers

By Family Status

Single
Married with no kids
Married parents
Working parents
Stay-at-home parents

Step-parents
Single parents
Divorced
Widowed

Try combining a couple of these and see what you come up with, for example: "middle aged surfers" or "single CEO's".

Exercise 4: What problems do you want to solve?

Next, ask yourself:

What issues are these people facing?

How can I support them?

What am I interested in studying?

Where have I gained life experience and how does that apply here?

For example, Mary has worked in human resources for large pharmaceutical companies. She has enjoyed this work but is wondering whether she could start consulting part time rather than working full time and start selling information products to bring in passive income. After reviewing her experience and reflecting on what she enjoys most, she sees that her biggest successes have been in resolving employee conflicts. The problem she will solve: "employee conflicts reduce productivity and lead to losing key staff".

Betty has been a nurse caring for patients with life-threatening diseases, particularly those with cancer. As she looks back over her career and reflects on what she has enjoyed most, she sees that some of her best work has involved supporting the *families* of the ill patients and teaching these families to provide real support to the patient. The problem she will solve: "when your loved one is dying, it's hard to know the right thing to do".

Paul has several close women friends who have been through divorce. Time and again, they have turned to him for support throughout the process, and he has become quite familiar with the stages women go through in the process of divorce as well as appreciative of the strength it takes for women to make this transition. He feels that some of his best "work" has been to support these friends through their transition of going from being divorced to single. The problem he chooses to work with: "divorced women are having trouble standing on their own two feet and are finding it a really scary process".

What work and life problems have you solved, and how could these apply to what you are about to offer now?

Bonus Exercise 5: Ask your friends

If you're still a little fuzzy after the above exercises, set up a phone call or send an email to at least five people and ask:

Who do you believe I've helped the most?

What groups do you see me helping?

What problems do you see me solving?

What problems have you seen me solve or overcome in my own life?

How have I most helped you?

This will give you at least a very general idea of what you do well and who tends to value your work — in other words, your target market! Tip: phone, rather than email - you may find these conversations with your friends very rewarding.

The above exercises have everything you need to develop an exciting niche. However, if you'd like to delve into more advanced topics such as "Will they pay you?" and "Is there too much competition?", you can find resources on this topic at www.GetPaidForWhoYouAre.com/access.

Freedom Ninja says: Don't be daunted by the fact there may be many similar websites like the one that interests you out there. There were quite a number on personal finance when Trent Hamm started his (<u>www.thesimpledollar.com</u>), but his stands out and sparkles with energy.

Resource: Take Inventory Worksheet at <u>www.GetPaid For WhoYouAre.com/access</u>.

SECTION C
What To Put On Your Website

In Chapter 4 you examined how to set up a website in seven days. Here's more on what to put on your Welcome Page and your About Me/Contact Page.

CLEARLY STATING YOUR MISSION ON YOUR WELCOME PAGE

Let's start with who you help and the problems you solve. You may be able to cover both in one shot. For example, if you help women 45 and over move through divorce, you could say:

Are you losing sleep over your divorce?

Are you wondering how to get half the assets without a battle?

Do you want to keep custody of your kids?

From reading these questions, a woman considering divorce would know from a 3-second glance at your site that she's in the right place!

Or, you might phrase the problems you solve as statements. For example, if you were a career coach, you ask your site visitor to click if any of the following statements ring true:

I hate my job!

I've lost my direction and purpose.

I want more out of life.

Now it's your turn to write out the problems you solve. But before you do, pull out your worksheet on "the problems I solve and would like to solve" from Chapter 3, because you've done most of this work already. Refer back to your worksheet, select your top three problems and formulate them into questions or statements. These will go on your welcome page.

Next, you want to emphasize the benefits of working with you, such as more income, early retirement, divorce with ease and joy, or divorce while staying friends with your ex. You could write these up in bullet points — which are easier to read — or in one or two sentences. Take a few minutes to write out your benefits now.

Finally, write out what's unique and different about you. Don't worry about writing a full bio for now. Just focus on your unique selling proposition. In other words, why you? Do you have unique experience in your area? Or a good track record for success? Maybe you have handled special situations related to your niche? Are you super-passionate in this area?

Putting it all together, here's an example of home-page text:

Are you losing sleep over your divorce?
Are you wondering how to get half the assets without a battle?
Do you want to keep custody of your kids?

If so, you've come to the right place. At My Second Life, I help women 45 and over move powerfully through divorce and into the next wonderful and exciting phase of their lives. Some of the benefits my clients report are:

Peace of mind throughout the process
Staying friends with my ex while divorcing
Avoiding a custody battle
Getting the financial settlement I need

I myself have successfully survived divorce. And, seeing the impact it had on my partner who I still dearly love, I have a deep appreciation and respect for the strength it takes for women to make this transition, and I'd be honored to help you every step of the way.

SAYING WHO YOU ARE ON YOUR ABOUT ME/ CONTACT PAGE

Below is a sample bio that anyone without any kind of track record could use. Any concrete results or training you can add would make it even better:

> *"I have spent a lifetime searching for the keys to being happy and to living a life full of joy, passion and peace. Today, I am happy to say that I get to live a truly delightful life, with fabulous relationships, work I am passionate about and the confidence that I can achieve anything. My mission is to share with others what I have learned about creating your dreams and how to love the ride."*

This is also the page where you'll put your contact information so people can reach you. If you have it, include a nice friendly headshot (remember, the professional shots can come later). Add your Twitter and Facebook address if you have them, and if not, don't worry about it.

You can also use the About Me/Contact page to suggest why people might *want* to contact you. For example, "Contact me:

- For a free article on the top five mistakes women make while getting divorced
- For a free 30-minute consultation
- To find out more about my programs and fees
- To subscribe to the My Second Life monthly newsletter"

List three to four reasons why people might want to contact you and add your email address and phone number (if you have one you don't mind being public).

Resource: For a form and sample bios to help you generate ideas, download the *10 Sample Bios* form and the *Create My Bio* form at www.GetPaidForWhoYouAre.com/access.

SECTION D
Search Engine Optimization —
More on How to Get Massive Traffic

Know this: no traffic equals no profits.

Unless you know how to drive a lot of traffic to your website, it will remain one of the millions of unfindable could-have-been sites.

Freedom Ninja Tip: Strap yourself in here because the going is, by necessity, going to get a little technical. That's why it's here in the back of the book where you can easily refer to it as often as you need.

In Chapter 7 we covered several strategies to generate traffic to your site and gave a brief outline of Search Engine Optimization (SEO). Let's go into more detail on the four basic steps required for good SEO:

1) Pick your keywords
2) Create and Optimize your pages
3) Get links to your site (by writing articles!)
4) Create more pages for your site

1) PICK YOUR KEYWORDS

The words a person is searching for on Google are sometimes called "keywords". If your target market is women over 40 in some kind of transition, how can they find you? What keywords or keyphrases would such women put in a search engine to find you? What would they type into the Google box? What are they seeking?

This section is about working out what those keywords might be. Once you have those, you will focus in on your top ten keywords and then craft or optimize your website so that your site ranks highly in the search engines for those terms.

If you just said, "I'm going to help women. I just coach women" then good luck getting to the top of Google with just the keyword "women." If you type "women" into Google, you will get 635 million results — do you really want to compete against those?

You have to be more specific so that you're competing with fewer people. If you put "women in transition," into Google, you get 14.4 million results, and "women in transition Dallas," gets 114,000 results. Do you see how by focusing on more specific terms (also known as 'long tail' keywords) we are weeding out competition and giving ourselves a fighting chance?

To take it further, transitions can take place in relationships, and often around divorce, so that suggests the key phrases "women surviving divorce" and "women going through a divorce". Other key phrases could be "how to handle a new relationship", "how to handle a new job", "how to get a new job" and "women in a career change", with the word "Dallas" possibly being added to every one.

Google has a great tool for helping you research keywords. Type "Google keyword suggestion tool" into Google or use the link below. Type in your phrase — for example, "women in transition" then click "Get keyword ideas".

The tool will also tell you how much search volume there is for each keyword. There's no point putting up a page for a keyword that only has five searches a month. But if you can see that there are over 500 searches a month, it may be worth it.

Choose your top four keywords

Now that you've brainstormed and researched lots of possible keywords, narrow them down to your top four. This is as much an art as it is a science — I can't give you a magic formula. You'll need to find a balance between a) relevance, and b) achievability.

Relevance: choose terms that are most likely to generate paying customers for you because they are the exact words your ideal customer is likely to be searching on e.g. "stop my divorce Dallas" if you're a divorce coach in Dallas.

Achievability: I'd personally love to rank top ten for the word "divorce", but I don't have two years to invest in making it happen. So you'll pick some longer phrases that have less competition. Ideally, when you search on this term in Google, it will return less than 1 million results.

2) CREATE AND OPTIMIZE YOUR PAGES
Create four pages

Optimizing your website means making it search engine friendly, so that it can rank highly in the search engines for your chosen keywords.

The simplest course of action is: once you've chosen your keywords, create an article based on each one, then ask your

Web Wizard to make sure that those keywords appear in all the right places for Google. Once you've written the article, you can ask an expert from www.elance.com to help you optimize it. And I'll give you an outline here of how to do it.

In the example of women in transition finding you, you might create one page for each of the keyword phrases: "women in transition book", "women shelters", "women in crisis", and "transition community". You would do an article on "women in transition book", with that keyphrase appearing frequently on the page. Keep keyword frequency to under 5%, i.e., if you had 100 words on the page, the most it would appear is 5 times. Try to also use slightly different ways of saying it like "if you are looking for a book for women on transition" so it doesn't look artificial.

When you (or your Web Wizard) save the page, you should also include your keywords in the file name of the page. E.g., "womenintransitionbook.htm".

Put your keywords in the right spots

If you have bold text on your site, put your keywords there. Put them in the headings on your website. Put them in your title tags, content tags and description tags of your website, and in the "alternative text" field for images.

Also put your keywords in the actual text of the links on your site. You will likely have links on your page to other pages on your site and to other useful sites. Instead of just saying "Click here for more information", that's a great place to put a key phrase like "Women in transition". Google sees that it's a link to another page and therefore considers it more important than normal text.

The figure above shows the placement of coaching-related keywords on my home page.

I remind you too that another great place to have a strong keyword is in your domain (or website) name. If you already chose and registered a domain name then this is already handled. If you haven't, I suggest you review the section on "Register your website name" in Chapter 4, as keywords in your domain name will do a lot for your search engine rankings.

One more factor to consider is your site's navigation. You want to make sure that each page is linked to at least one other page on your site, as well as the home page. This is important because if each of your pages links back to the home page, then

Google decides that your home page must be pretty important and gives it a higher page rank.

3) GET LINKS TO YOUR SITE

You've now learned about onsite factors, which are what you can do with your Web pages. Now let's talk about offsite factors, which are what can you do outside your Web page to help bring in traffic. You have to have other websites link to you. You can have the best content in the world, but if no one's linking to you, Google won't believe you.

I used to think that you needed thousands of links to get to the top, but the latest information is you just need 30 to 50 links. If you have 30 to 50 links, then Google says, "Okay, we trust that you're a valid site." After that it's about your content, which is discussed in point 4.

Link exchange

Exchange links with other websites in your industry. Don't just exchange links with any site, or Google will say "Hang on, an auto mechanic site is linking to a site about cats? I don't buy it." Get links from websites in related industries, also known as "themed links".

When other people link to your site, make sure they do so in the right way. If the clickable text (also known as 'anchor text') in their link to your site says "Visit this site" that doesn't help you. Make sure that they use your keywords in their link. You want them to say, "Visit this comprehensive site about Dallas women in transition". The term "Dallas women in transition" will be highlighted and clickable, also called "hyperlinked", which gives you more credibility with Google.

> **Freedom Ninja Tip:** Another way to exchange links is through a link exchange program. They have a list of thousands of websites that want to trade links and have broken them down into categories. Pick 50-250 sites and approach them individually. Because they're already a member of the link exchange program, they just have to click a button and the link appears on their site and on your site. How's that for clever! You don't need this when you're getting started, but it's nice to know it's there when you're ready to ramp up.

One way to exchange links is to go to the top 50, 100, or 1,000 websites, depending on how motivated you are. Even better, get a college student to do this for $10 an hour. Or find someone in India to do link exchanges for $4 an hour, or less, using www.elance.com or www.rentacoder.com.

You or your link manager will approach a relevant website and say, "I'd like to get a higher ranking in Google and I'd like to help you too. Would you like to exchange links?" Try telephoning people instead of just emailing, because people generally ignore emails for link requests.

Write articles and post them

Another great way to get links is to write articles. You can post these articles for free on ezine sites, such as www.EzineMarketplace.com or www.Ezinearticles.com Each article centers on a particular keyword and links back to your website.

> Freedom Ninja says: If you're wondering where to focus your efforts, writing or obtaining articles is a good place. Some people focus 100% on this strategy to get links. They commit to writing an article every day for 30 days.

Either through link exchanges or article posting, spend 2-3 months getting 30 inbound links to your site.

4) CREATE MORE PAGES FOR YOUR SITE

Once you've got your first four Web pages up and 30 links coming into your site, it's time to add another 20 pages to your website, using keywords related to your content.

It used to be that you could have hundreds of links and rank high on Google's search pages, even if you only had a few pages of content. But now, Google wants to see a lot of content before it will consider your site credible.

So write 20 more articles and put them on your site, link them to your home page and post them on www.Ezinearticles.com to get a lot more links.

My site, www.life-coaching-resource.com, comes up top five in Google with the keywords "life coaching" partly due to over 300 pages of content. It didn't happen overnight, but you start small and build each week.

WHAT NOT TO DO

- Don't use computer-generated pages. Some software programs will search the Web and create "fake" pages of content around the keywords you have chosen. They sometimes fool the search engines, but don't always make sense to a real person. Google bans such websites.
- Don't try to fill your pages only with keywords, or hide keywords by putting them in the same color as the page background. Deceptive practices will get your site banned by Google.
- Don't create duplicate content. Your pages should contain original and significant content. Don't just copy content from other people's websites, unless you are adding value such as commentary or editorial.

In general, create valuable content that people will want to link to, and you'll attract traffic.

SECTION E
Partnering with Nonprofits and Corporations

This section builds on Chapter 8 and covers how to choose your nonprofit, how to approach the organization, and partnering with corporations.

HOW TO CHOOSE YOUR NONPROFIT

Here are some guidelines to consider:

Passion This is probably the most important consideration. You don't want to be on a radio show talking about a nonprofit you don't care about. People are going to feel it and you're going to feel it. So pick a nonprofit you care about.

Location If you're a coach or some kind of professional, you might be providing services nationally or worldwide, so you could go for a national nonprofit. But if you serve San Francisco businesses, then form a relationship with a nonprofit in San Francisco rather than going for the national organization.

Even if you are national, it can be easier to do something small with a local chapter, build a relationship with them and then leverage it later into something bigger with the national organization.

Target Market Choose a nonprofit that is working with the same target market you are. For example, Brendon Burchard wrote a book called *Life's Golden Ticket*, and he's passionate about youth. He thought, "This book could be really great for youth, so who serves youth?" He went to the YMCA, Kiwanis and Junior Achievement, who reach 30 million people combined, and partnered with those organizations at the national level.

If you're a fitness coach, fitness trainer, health coach or nutritional counselor, ask yourself what nonprofits focus on health? There's the American Heart Association, the American Cancer Society and thousands of smaller ones that are much more accessible.

Example: If you help people to start their own business, you might be trying to reach people with some formal education, who are a little cyber savvy. One possible partnership target might be www.Kiva.org. We could assume their donor base is people with money because they're giving money to Kiva to help small entrepreneurs in third world countries. They are also likely to be professionals and are probably a bit more tech savvy, because Kiva is a hip, happening tech-based nonprofit.

Brand Recognition All other things being equal, choose someone with a recognized brand. You don't really want a startup unless you think they're going to start-up big and fast. You want an organization that people will recognize. When you call the local radio station and say, "I'm doing this thing to benefit so-and-so in a partnership and I wonder if you would like to hear about it" obviously it's better if the station recognizes the nonprofit organization's name.

Size If you're choosing between two nonprofits who are both willing to work with you and one's got an email list of 2,000 people and the other one's got an email list of 25,000 people, obviously you'll go with the larger one.

What you're trying to do is to find the biggest nonprofit you can, that you really care about, that is willing to work with you. Perhaps you ask several nonprofits and they all say, "No, we don't know who you are, you're too small". So, you might go for some really tiny ones just to get started. Build your practice and get a little bit of media exposure. The media might go for it because it's a nice story about a small company helping a startup nonprofit.

Again, don't go to the national level of a big nonprofit unless you have a lot of credibility or big partners behind you. Start with a local chapter and hit a home run with them. Volunteer for them, get to know them, offer to partner with just that chapter and do a good job. Then leverage that to the national level.

To find potential nonprofit partners, go to www.CharityNavigator.com. You can search by using keywords, such as "homeless organizations" and it'll bring up numerous homeless organizations that they've rated. You can also look up references at your local library, or Google something like "homeless charity Detroit".

My Example: Six months ago I came up with an idea for a global campaign that would attract a lot of online traffic and media attention. I went to a lot of big nonprofits: Sierra Club, Red Cross, American Heart Association, World Vision, Habitat for Humanity, UNICEF, and a string of others.

Organizations were interested, even at the national level, because my project was a really good idea and it had been done once before, so it was a proven concept. Plus I had some credibility behind me — I'd built a following of 70,000 subscribers, had some media credits and Jack Canfield from *Chicken Soup for the Soul* was writing the foreword to my book.

I got through to six different departments at Microsoft, two executive vice presidents at AARP, several vice presidents at The American Cancer Society and a senior marketing executive at Delta Airlines. This last executive told me: "It's as good as, if not better, than, any sponsorship proposal I've ever seen".

Resource: You can download this proposal, and the simpler one I ended up using for the book launch, at www.GetPaidForWhoYouAre.com/access.

But in the end I couldn't find any confirmed partners because I was aiming too high for someone who hadn't proven himself with that particular project. So I switched to a much smaller project involving no cash and focusing on a simple book launch and had instant success.

I approached some partners saying: "We're going to launch my book to a lot of people online. I'd like to get you in front of that audience and raise funds and awareness for you. We'll put you in the book. We'll ask people to donate. We'll put you on the website. We'll help build your mailing list and I'll mention you on any TV appearances I do."

It was simple. They got it, they liked it, and they said "yes".

HOW TO APPROACH A NONPROFIT ORGANIZATION

Do your research

When approaching a nonprofit, you'll want to answer these two questions:

What is its mission?

What is its main focus for the next 12 months? (More funds? More volunteers? More awareness? More newsletter subscribers?)

The first question can be answered on their website. Armed with this, call the Director of Development (often listed on the website) and ask the second question.

Elements of a proposal

The strongest proposals require very little from a nonprofit, yet promise to raise funds and awareness. An attractive proposal:

- Requires no money from them
- Requires little time from them
- Provides a guaranteed minimum in dollars raised
- Is easy to do
- Supports ("ties-in with") a project *they are already doing*

Most nonprofits are stretched. They have small budgets and very few staff. The best proposals do not stretch these limited resources more. They might put a little work into it if there is a lot of potential, but the less you require, the stronger your proposal will be. Once you have built a relationship with an organization, you might propose future campaigns that require more investment on their part, but not until you have created a track record with them.

They're also looking for simplicity. You don't want something that is complicated, has lots of moving parts, requires lots of coordination and that you have never done before — no matter how brilliant it may seem. A complex plan takes too long for people to understand and it's too much work. Stick to a simple plan.

When you craft a proposal for the organization, you want to support its existing goals and projects. If your proposal ties in with their existing plans, it is much more likely to be accepted. You will be able to say, "I'd like to use my business as a tool to help you do that." But if your proposal is to *add* another project to their plate, it's going to be much harder to get a yes.

Contact the Director of Development

Once you've done your research and planned your proposal, contact the fundraising director at the organization. You can go to its website, which might list staff members. You generally want to find the "Director of Development" since "development" means fundraising. If you can't find that person on the website, call and ask for the Director of Development.

Be prepared to present the idea on the phone immediately (the 2-5 minute version) if the director is open to it.

Here's a typical conversation:

You: *"Hi, my name is _____. I'm a professional _____, in the local business area. I'd like to use my business as a tool to raise funds and awareness for you. I'm wondering when would be a good time to spend just five to ten minutes talking about that?"*

Director: *"How about now?"*

You: *"Great. I'm launching a cool new product and I'd like to give you 50 percent of the purchase price for every one of your supporters who buys it."*

Director: *"What would you need from us to do this?"*

You: *"I'd just like you to help get the word out about this launch and our partnership."*

Director: *"How would it work?"*

You start explaining your proposal further. After you have done so, you can ask:

How big is your email list?

How many people do you reach via email?

How many people do you reach via direct mail?

Do you have a sense of how much web traffic you have?

This will give you a sense of the reach of this nonprofit and if they would be a suitable partner for you.

PARTNERING WITH CORPORATIONS

This chapter is focused mainly on partnering with nonprofits. However, that's just the beginning. All the skills you learned above can be applied to partnering with a local business or a global corporation. And — they have money!

Corporations like to be associated with the good work nonprofits are doing. They also want to reach the nonprofit's supporter base.

Corporations are trying to either reinforce their brand or change their brand image. And of course they want sales. Traditional advertising methods aren't working as well as they used to, because everyone is continually bombarded with advertising messages. Companies want new, hip ideas that will give their customers a valuable experience to associate with their brand.

For example, one of my book launch partners wanted people to associate their product with the experience of inspiration and excitement from creating a lifestyle of freedom and contribution. My readers will see the sponsor's logo on the book website, read about the sponsor in the book, and learn about special offers from the sponsor via my email newsletters later on. For a corporation, that type of marketing penetrates much more deeply than a simple television or newspaper ad that people won't trust and may ignore.

Organizations need you. They can't come up with all the ideas, and they can't create the content. They can't write this book you're reading or organize a book launch. They have a million other things to do. They need people just like you to approach them with compelling content and ideas that will reach a target market they are interested in.

U.S. corporations spend more than $13 billion a year on sponsorships. More than 2 million U.S. nonprofits receive $260 billion in donations[1]. Wouldn't you be happy with just a tiny slice of the pie?

1 www.nonprofitcareerguide.org/fact_sheet-scope.php
Data is drawn from Kennard T. Wing, Thomas H. Pollak, Amy Blackwood, and Linda M. Lampkin, The Nonprofit Almanac 2008 (Washington, DC: The Urban Institute Press, forthcoming); and Thomas H. Pollack and Amy Blackwood, The Nonprofit Sector in Brief: Facts and Figures from the Nonprofit Almanac 2007 (Washington, D.C.: National Center for Charitable Statistics at the Urban Institute); available at www.urban.org.)

Corporate sponsors can provide:

- Credibility
- Cash
- Publicity (get you on talk shows, arrange interviews, issue press releases)
- Access to their staff and customers
- Exposure on their website
- Payment for advertising
- In-kind sponsorship (For example, www.GoDaddy.com might build your website; Delta Airlines might give you airline tickets; Yahoo might give you advertising)

Can you imagine having a reputable nonprofit AND a corporation backing you? The three of you could really make a beautiful partnership. Nonprofits are used to partnering with corporations. You can bring them a three-way partnership, with you in the middle!

Author and speaker Brendon Burchard, who first inspired me with this partnership model, has had amazing success using these methods. He has partnered with nonprofits and corporations, including Wachovia, Walmart, Sony Pictures, Disney, Junior Achievement, YMCA and Kiwanis.

Here are some of the things Brendon has achieved through these partnerships:

- $370,000 in foreign advance sales of his book *Life's Golden Ticket* (as a first time author!)
- $500,000 in revenue for his first seminar, the College Success Boot Camp
- 67 speeches, 14 major fundraisers, in 12 countries
- 42 city sponsor-funded book tour
- $250,000 raised for his favorite cause

PRODUCTS AND SERVICES

These are the types of products and services that can be promoted through a partnership.

- Live seminars or events
- Training programs
- Teleseminars
- Teleclass series
- Books
- Services (e.g., Coaching Services)
- Contests or Sweepstakes
- Product Launches
- Causes

FURTHER PARTNERSHIP TRAINING

If you're as excited as I am about the possibilities around partnering with nonprofits and corporations, I highly recommend Brendon Burchard's Partnership Seminar. I've attended it twice and I'm now a bit of an evangelist for the training. Just know up front — it takes work to apply this model. You can't just start today and expect that you'll have a big partnership in a week. But out of all the ways you can market your business, I think this is one of the most powerful and rewarding there is.

Resource: Brendon Burchard's Partnership Seminar training: www.GoPartnershipSeminar.com

SECTION F
Continuing Education Program

I trust this book will get you off to a powerful start. Set up your Freedom Buddy for support, schedule time to follow the action steps and actually do them. That's what it takes for success.

And, I'm a strong believer in continuing education. Now that you have the foundation for the Five Freedom Steps, it's helpful to have a place to turn for support, advice, and further detail on *how to implement* the steps. I encourage you to continue your education to support your success in your online business. If you'd like to continue with the strategies in this book, I recommend Get Paid University. It's where I've put everything that I couldn't possibly fit in this book, including forms, worksheets, training videos, expansion modules and even three bonus online chapters.

Below is a partial list of the resources you'll find in the different membership levels of Get Paid University, bearing in mind that it keeps expanding.

STEP 1) DECIDE WHO YOU HELP
- "Take Inventory" Worksheet
- "Decide WHO You Help" Expansion Module
- "Define Your Market" worksheet
- Training audio plus transcript

STEP 2) SET UP YOUR WEBSITE IN 7 DAYS
- Sample Bios
- "Create My Bio" Form

- Bonus Online Chapter: "Creating Coaching or Consulting Revenue, for strategies on how to sell coaching or consulting from your site"
- "Web Wizard Hiring Guide" (including a sample ad you can post)
- "Web Host Support Guide" — for a review of the major hosting services
- "How to Create a Website in 7 Days" Expansion Module
- Training audio plus transcript

STEP 3) SET UP YOUR NEWSLETTER IN 7 DAYS

- "Freebie in a Flash" form, which will guide you quickly through creating your own freebie
- "Friends Into Subscribers" Scripts for sample text you can send to your existing network to invite them to subscribe
- Links to free newsletter template sites, plus download and use the text template I started with
- "How to Easily Produce Newsletters" Guide
- "10 Newsletters In A Flash" Worksheet to create 10 quick newsletters
- "Create Your Newsletter" Expansion Module for further tips and strategies
- Training audio plus transcript

STEP 4) CREATE YOUR OWN PRODUCT IN 7 DAYS

- Sample four-week teleclass series structure
- List of recommended credit card merchant accounts
- "Product Promotion Strategies" Special Report
- Training audio plus transcript

STEP 5) GET MASSIVE TRAFFIC

- Expansion Module: "How to Get Massive Traffic" — for more on getting traffic
- "Pay Per Click Advertising Strategies" Report
- "Speaker Feedback Form" — a ninja form I use to collect leads and email subscribers at a speech
- Extended interview with wine blogger Brian Johnson
- Training audio plus transcript

GIVE AND GROW YOUR BUSINESS

- Book Launch Sponsorship Proposal
- Sponsorship Proposal to Delta Airlines
- Training audio plus transcript

ONLINE BONUS CHAPTERS

- *Bonus Chapter 10:* Building a Massive Email List — for even more advanced methods of getting traffic and building your email list
- *Bonus Chapter 11:* Add a Coaching or Consulting Revenue Stream

- *Bonus Chapter 12:* Borrowing Someone Else's Product — a look at affiliate marketing and expanding your product funnel using what others have created

As an owner of 'Get Paid For Who You Are™', you qualify for a free month's membership of Get Paid University. Visit www.GetPaidForWhoYouAre.com/access and use the code "freedom".

ACKNOWLEDGEMENTS

Thank you, Kristina, for encouraging me to write the book people were asking for, instead of the book I wanted them to ask for.

Thanks Mum and Dad for doing countless things right.

Thank you, Beth, for always keeping things running so I get to do what I do.

Thanks to Tim Ferriss for making me jealous enough to write the damn book, Jack Canfield for generously writing the foreword so I could shamelessly use his name more often than my own, Seth Godin for helping me stick to my guns, Russ Hall for some awesome re-writing, Stewart Emery for valuable direction, Flaven for throwing me a rope when I was free falling, Bernie and Ezra for who they be, Diana for inspiring the title, and my R&D team for loads of feedback and advice — with special mentions to Lori Smith, Maria Andreu, Joshua Aragon, Corrie-Anne Gray, Sharon Stidham and Michael Ellsberg.

And while it's not the done thing at all, I thank myself for sticking with it for 30 months, turning down publishing offers that didn't feel right, and putting everything I had into it — sink or swim.

ABOUT THE AUTHOR

David Wood is fast becoming one of the foremost voices in online marketing and lifestyle design, having built a rewarding hobby into a million-dollar online empire that allows him to work and play from anywhere in the world. He was recently voted into the Transformational Leadership Council, along with such thought leaders as Stephen M.R. Covey, Jack Canfield, John Gray, and Marianne Williamson.

In 1997, while consulting to Fortune 100 companies in New York, David felt the call to resign as an actuary and follow his passion to entertain and teach. Within a few short years he was attracting 95% of his clients from the internet, publishing the largest online coaching newsletter in the world, and celebrating reaching seven figures in income — all supported by one employee he'd never met.

He wrote *Get Paid For Who You Are*™ to share the same techniques he has now taught to thousands of people around the world, including students at Columbia University. Born in Australia, David has a home base in San Francisco and spends time in Calgary, New York, and Sydney.